THE CROCHET ANSWER BOOK

The
Crochet
Answer Book

EDIE ECKMAN

Storey Publishing

*The mission of Storey Publishing is to serve our customers by
publishing practical information that encourages
personal independence in harmony with the environment.*

Edited by Gwen Steege and Sarah Guare
Cover and text design by Kent Lew
Text production by Jen Rork Design
Production assistance by Jennifer Jepson Smith
Illustrations by © Brigita Fuhrmann
Indexed by Christine R. Lindemer, Boston Road Communications

The information in this book is true and complete to the best of our knowledge.
All recommendations are made without guarantee on the part of the author or
Storey Publishing. The author and publisher disclaim any liability in connection
with the use of this information. For additional information please contact
Storey Publishing, 210 MASS MoCA Way, North Adams, MA 01247.

Storey books are available for special premium and promotional uses and for
customized editions. For further information, please call 1-800-793-9396.

Printed in China by R.R. Donnelley
10 9 8 7 6 5 4

Library of Congress Cataloging-in-Publication Data

Eckman, Edie.
    The crochet answer book / by Edie Eckman.
        p. cm.
    Includes index.
    ISBN-13: 978-1-58017-598-2 (pbk. : alk. paper)
    1. Crocheting—Miscellanea. I. Title.

TT820.E35 2005
746.43'4—dc22
                                                        2005016484

To Bill, Meg, and Charlie, for their unwavering support and for not complaining about another restaurant meal, and to Tyler, for keeping me company

Contents

ACKNOWLEDGEMENTS

Thanks to all the authors and teachers who answered my questions and to my students, who asked them.

Thanks to Mom, for reading the whole book; to Janice and Sally, for their help; and to webmaster Charlie for doing it, even when I know how.

Special thanks to Gwen for taking the time to learn more about crochet and remaining cheerful, and to Brigita and Ilona for drawing and re-drawing until we got it right.

All You Have to Do Is Ask!

OFTEN I'M STRUCK by how frequently crocheters qualify their skills by following the words "I crochet" with "but I'm not very good." When questioned closely, crocheters tend to harbor similar insecurities about where to put the hook, how to maintain the required number of stitches, how to determine gauge, and how to read a pattern.

In my opinion, being a "good" crocheter is not about making perfectly stitched, elaborate, artful creations. It is rather a matter of confidence. You need to be sure of what you are doing and how to do it, and then have the confidence to figure out what to do if things aren't going quite right. Understanding why you do certain things and why they turn out the way they do increases confidence and leads to successful crocheting.

Wouldn't it boost your confidence to have an experienced and confident crocheter on call, day and night, offering assistance when needed? Most of us aren't fortunate enough to have that kind of aid, but I'm hoping this book will serve that purpose for you. I've tried to answer some of the most common questions crocheters have and to anticipate some questions you didn't know you had. There are different ways to do almost everything; I may have left something unsaid; and perhaps I have even omitted your most burning question! If I have left something out, I'd love to hear about your unanswered questions or how you have solved your own problems.

If you cared enough to pick up this book, you are either my mother or are at least mildly interested in crochet. I don't really expect anyone (except my mom) to read the book cover-to-cover. Instead, I hope you'll visit it from time to time to answer questions as they come up. Whatever your personal hang-up, flip to the section of this book that addresses your questions, open your mind, pick up yarn and hook, and give crocheting a try.

It is my hope that *The Crochet Answer Book* will lead you down the road to gaining the confidence that makes for good crocheting.

CHAPTER 1

Get a Grip . . . on Hooks and Other Tools

ONE NICE THING ABOUT CROCHET is that you need only two things: a hook and yarn. Of course, there are many other useful tools and accessories that can make your crocheting life more enjoyable. Let's explore some of the many options on the market, beginning with the hook.

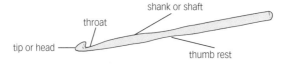

shank or shaft

throat

tip or head

thumb rest

All about Hooks

Q What are the differences among hooks?

A Hooks are made of plastic, metal, wood, nylon, or bone. Some have a thumb rest; others have a straight shank with no thumb rest. The handle may be cushioned or shaped. Some have an inline head while others have a tapered head with a tapered throat. When you crochet with thread, you use a steel hook

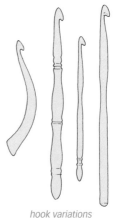

hook variations

that may be so tiny that you can barely see the shape of
the head.

And those are just the regular hooks! There are also spe-
cialty hooks. Hooks used for Tunisian crochet have a long
straight shank that resembles a knitting needle. Double-
ended hooks have a hook at each end of a long straight shank.

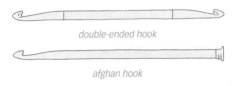

double-ended hook

afghan hook

Q **With all the choices available, how do I know which
hook is best?**

A Choose the style hook that is most comfortable for
your hand. It should be of good quality, with no rough
spots. Some people prefer to work with a certain brand of
hook or with hooks made from a certain material. And, of
course, the size of the hook should be appropriate for the
yarn or thread you are using. No matter what type of hook
you have, the shank is the major determining factor in the
size of the stitch.

You may find that you prefer different types of hooks for
different yarns and stitch patterns. Slippery yarns like rayon
might be easier to manage with a "sticky" wooden hook,

while fuzzy yarns might work up faster when you use a slick aluminum hook.

....

Q How are hooks sized?

A Hook sizes can be described in US or metric terms. Often US terms include both letters and numbers. Standard crochet hooks range from US size B/1 (2.25 mm) through jumbo size S (19 mm). But beware! Hook sizes may vary from manufacturer to manufacturer. There is no guarantee that one company's size H (5 mm) hook is the same size as another company's, even when both are described in metric terms. In addition, numbering systems have changed over time, even with hooks from the same manufacturer. It is always best to use a hook gauge to determine the size of your hook in metric terms.

SEE ALSO: *Page 21 for description of hook gauge.*

Q What size hook do I need?

A When you follow a published pattern, the instructions suggest a size, but this is only a starting point. You still need to work a swatch to check your gauge. If you need to change from the suggested hook size in order to get correct gauge then by all means do so. Having the correct gauge is always more important than using the suggested hook size.

Hook Sizes

This chart is a compilation of hook and size ranges from various sources. Keep in mind that the great variation of numbering systems over the years can greatly confuse things. For example, a comparison of hook charts from a number of sources lists a 4.0 mm hook as either a G/6 or an F/5.

METRIC	US
.60 mm	14 steel
.75	14 steel
.85	13 steel
1.00	12 steel
1.1	11 steel
1.25	
1.3	10 steel
1.4	9 steel
1.5	8 steel
1.65	7 steel
1.75, 1.8	6 steel
1.9	5 steel
2.0	4 steel
2.1	3 steel
2.25	2 steel, B/1
2.5, 2.75	C/2
3.0, 3.25	D/3
3.5	E/4
3.75, 4.0	F/5
4.0, 4.25	G/6
4.5	7
5	H/8
5.5	I/9
6.0	J/10
6.5, 7.0	K/10.5
8	L/11
9	M, N /13
10	N, P /15
15	P, Q
16	Q
19	S

Note: *The steel hooks used for thread crochet have their own numbering system ranging from a tiny US size 14 (.75 mm) through a still small-ish US size E/4 (3.5 mm).*

If you aren't following a published pattern, you need to match the hook to the yarn or thread you are using: Larger yarns require larger hooks. Most yarn labels suggest an appropriate-sized hook for that yarn.

SEE ALSO: *See pages 124–25, for working a swatch; and pages 34–35, Yarn Weights with Recommended Hook Sizes and Gauges.*

Q **How do I hold the hook?**

A Hold the hook in your dominant hand in the way that is most comfortable for you. The most common ways to hold a hook are shown below. If you hold the hook a different way from those shown, and it works for you, then don't feel you must change your technique.

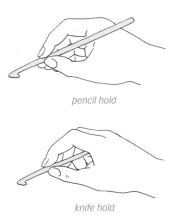

pencil hold

knife hold

Q How do I hold the yarn?

A The yarn from the ball needs to be tensioned through the fingers of the hand not holding the hook. The end of the yarn attached to the hook goes over your forefinger. The yarn should move freely through your fingers, while still

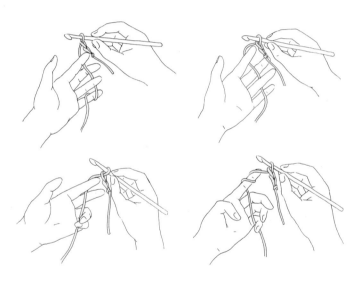

various ways to hold yarn

Note: *In these illustrations, the hand holding the yarn is shown palm up so that you can see the path of the yarn. When you are stitching, you should close your hand over the yarn so that you hold it with your palm down.*

being within your control. You may want to wrap it under and over other fingers in addition to your forefinger, or wrap it twice around your forefinger or pinkie. Experiment with ways to tension the yarn so that it is comfortable for you. Don't worry if it feels awkward at first — with practice it will feel more natural.

Some people choose to hold both the yarn and the hook in their dominant hand, and throw the yarn over the hook as if they are knitting. If you do this and you are comfortable with it, that's fine, but if you are just starting out it's worth learning to tension the yarn through the fingers of your other hand.

Q **My mother and my friend hold the hook and yarn differently. Which way is correct?**

A Neither is the only correct technique. It's okay to hold the hook and the yarn in any way that is comfortable to you, even if it's not one of the ways illustrated here. As long as you are happy with the consistency of the stitches and are comfortable while you are crocheting, you are correct.

Q **When I crochet for more than an hour, my hands start to ache. Is there anything I can do to keep them from hurting?**

A   There are a number of precautions you can take to prevent injuries from cutting into your crocheting time:

▶ Start with a hook that is comfortable for you. You may enjoy using a hook with a cushioned handle or a specially shaped grip. Hold the hook and yarn gently, and try varying the way you hold them. If you normally use the pencil hold, try the knife hold at least some of the time.

▶ Support your shoulders and back — don't slouch! Allow your work to rest on your lap so that you aren't holding its weight with your hands. Support your arms and elbows while you stitch.

▶ Some yarns are harder on the hands than others; stay away from inelastic cotton, silk, and linen if they cause problems.

▶ Take frequent breaks to rest and stretch. Stretch your fingers out as far as possible for a count of ten, and then make a clenched fist for a count of ten. Repeat this several times. Rotate your wrists clockwise, then counterclockwise. Shrug your shoulders up and down, and in circles.

▶ Therapeutic gloves may help. You can find these at craft stores and yarn shops.

▶ Most important, if you experience tingling or numbness in your hands, or if you have persistent discomfort, stop and consult a health-care professional. Crocheting should never hurt.

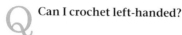

Q Can I crochet left-handed?

A Certainly! Hold the hook in your left hand and the yarn in your right hand, and stitch from left to right, instead of right to left.

If you are learning from a right-handed crocheter, or following a published pattern, you may have to make some adjustments, as most instructions are written for a predominantly right-handed world. If a right-hander is teaching you to crochet, sit opposite her and mimic her actions; you'll be crocheting left-handed. Some books contain illustrations for both right- and left-handed stitchers. You can follow illustrations for right-handed crochet by holding a mirror to the side of the illustration, or by scanning the illustration into your computer and flipping it horizontally on a graphics program. (*Note:* To avoid copyright infringement, make copies for your own use only.) Because you are working from left to right, the shaping of some pieces will take place on the "other" side of the garment. In other words, if you follow cardigan instructions for the Right Front, you'll be making the Left Front.

You may find that you can work just fine holding the hook in your right hand as right-handers do. If you can, just stitch "right-handed."

Filling Your Tool Bag

Q **What other tools do I need?**

A Although a crochet hook and scissors are really the only tools you must have, a number of others are useful. You may want to keep a little tool bag handy, filled with some or all of these other practical tools:

▶ **Small, sharp scissors.** These come in many styles. Keeping them at hand saves time and frustration.

▶ **Tapestry needles.** Also called yarn needles, these blunt-tipped sewing needles have large eyes. They come in several sizes; you'll want at least two sizes to correspond to the size of the yarns and threads you use most often.

▶ **Measuring tools.** You'll be less tempted to cheat on measurements if you keep a tape measure and a ruler at hand. A tape measure is good for measuring bodies; a ruler is best for measuring flat fabrics.

▶ **Hook gauge.** Use a metal hook gauge to determine the size of unmarked hooks. The hook gauge contains a series of holes in graduated sizes. The holes are numbered in both metric and US terms. Slide the shank of your hook into the smallest hole it fits, then read the corresponding number to determine the size of the hook.

▶ **Plastic stitch markers.** Available in a variety of styles, markers work better than pieces of yarn to mark stitches, as yarn can leave unwanted bits of fuzz in your fabric. Avoid the round markers meant only for knitting; you need a type that can be opened so you can hang it on a stitch.

stitch marker with opening

▶ **Coilfree safety pins.** Similar to safety pins, but without the yarn-grabbing circle at the far end, these little beauties are useful for marking stitches, holding pieces together for seaming, or keeping track of increases and decreases.

coilfree pin

▶ **"Personal discomfort fixers."** Hand lotion, lip balm, and a nail file can prevent annoying interruptions to your stitching sessions.

▶ **A calculator.** This is an important tool if you are doing your own designing, or adapting another's design. If you are always a strict pattern-follower, you may leave this one out of your bag.

▶ **Note-taking tools.** Keep a pen or pencil and paper handy to remind yourself where you are and what you have done. Get into the habit of making notes to yourself as you work. You may need to repeat something (or avoid it) later.

▶ **A row counter.** This comes in handy when row counts are important and you are working a stitch pattern that is difficult to keep track of, or when you are using a fuzzy yarn that just defies counting. You may also want to use it when working sleeve shaping, or to ensure you have the same number of rows on the left and right fronts of a cardigan.

▶ **A variety of crochet hooks in different sizes.** If you have alternatives near at hand, you are more likely to keep swatching until you get the right gauge.

SEE ALSO: *Pages 124–25, for swatching.*

▶ **A latch hook.** Use this great little tool for weaving in ends too short or too bulky to fit into a yarn needle.

latch hook

 I'm really into crochet. Are there any other tools that make the work easier and even more fun?

 There's always something more! Ask for these great tools for your next birthday:

▶ **Magnifying glasses/reading glasses.** If you are a certain age, and haven't yet discovered the joy of reading glasses for close work and small print, give these a try. Yarn and craft stores also carry magnifying glasses on a stand, or ones that hang around your neck and rest against your chest.

▶ **A ball winder and yarn swift.** These tools, used

together or separately, are wonderful time savers for winding hanks of yarn into flat, center-pull balls. You can also use the ball winder to rewind your yarn if you have to rip out a large expanse of stitching.

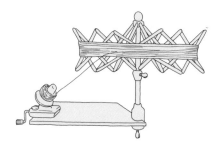

ball winder and yarn swift

▶ **Daylight lamp.** This is a special light bulb that emits full spectrum light. These bulbs can help you choose colors and make it easier to see dark stitches in the evening. Some companies make a combination lamp and magnifying glass.

▶ **Hook cases.** Use these to corral and organize your hooks. Unfortunately, it's still up to you to put them away when you are finished!

▶ **Pompom maker.** Pompom makers are an inexpensive luxury. You can certainly make pompoms using cardboard circles, but if you are going to make a lot of them, pompom makers are a treat.

CHAPTER 2

A Good Yarn

LUCKILY FOR US, there is a seemingly endless variety of yarns on today's market. However, with this diversity comes the matter of choice — which yarn is best for which types of projects? Understanding the characteristics of various yarns will help you determine the answer.

Kinds of Yarn

Q **What is yarn made of?**

A Animal, plant, and synthetic fibers are all used to make yarn. The animal fibers include silk produced by worms, wool from sheep, alpaca from alpacas, quiviut from the musk ox, angora from rabbits, and mohair from angora goats (go figure!). Plant fibers include cotton from cotton bolls, linen from the flax plant, and ramie from an Asian shrub. There are also yarns made from soy, bamboo, pine, and other plants. Acrylic, nylon, polyester and other synthetic fibers are man-made, in some cases from recycled materials. Lyocell (Tencel) and rayon are man-made fibers produced from cellulose, which is a natural material. "Metallic" yarns are usually a synthetic, metallic-looking fiber spun with another fiber.

What are some of the common terms used to describe yarn characteristics?

 All of the following terms will help you understand and describe the yarns you work with:

Absorbency. The ability of the fiber to take in water

Breathability. The ability of the fiber to allow air to pass through it

Dyeability. The ability of the fiber to accept and hold dye

Hand/handle. The way a fiber feels, a tactile description that may include words like: soft, fine, harsh, stiff, resilient. The hand of a fiber influences the hand of the fabric that it is made into; the fabric might additionally be described by its "drape."

SEE ALSO: *Pages 164–65, for drapeability.*

Loft. The amount of air between the fibers; lofty yarn is usually lighter in weight than its thickness implies. "Fuzzy" yarn is lofty.

Resiliency (elasticity). The ability of a fiber to return to its original shape after being stretched or pulled.

Thickness. The diameter of the fiber, measured in tiny units called microns.

 Why does fiber content matter?

 A yarn's characteristics, such as its resiliency, hand, loft, absorbency, and dyeability, are largely determined

by the fibers that make up that yarn. Knowing the fiber content of a yarn is also important when it comes time to launder your finished project.

Being familiar with the features of different fibers helps you make appropriate selections when you choose yarn for a project. You might decide, for instance, that while a luxurious alpaca throw is an excellent choice for your mother, a washable acrylic-blend yarn is a more suitable choice for your four-year-old son's afghan.

. . . .

Q What are fiber blends?

A Often fibers are blended to take advantage of the best properties of each one. For example, acrylic might be blended with wool to make the yarn machine washable, while maintaining the breathability of the wool fiber. A 50% alpaca/50% wool blend maintains the luxurious feel of the alpaca but is more affordable and more resilient than a 100% alpaca yarn.

The fiber with the higher percentage of content in the yarn dominates the yarn's characteristics. A 80% cotton/20% wool blend looks like a cotton yarn, but is lighter weight than a similar, all-cotton yarn would be.

. . . .

Q How is yarn made?

A The initial processing depends on the fiber. Wool, mohair, and alpaca are shorn from the animals, resulting in a fleece made up of staples (short strands similar to locks of hair). Angora rabbits are combed or clipped to remove their hair. Cotton bolls that look somewhat like the cotton balls in your bathroom cabinet are harvested from cotton plants and processed through a gin to remove the seeds. Silk comes off the cocoon of a silkworm in a continuous filament; these filaments may be cut into manageable lengths before they are processed. To make rayon, cellulose from wood or cotton is processed into a solution called viscose and then extruded through tiny nozzles to form the rayon fiber. Tencel is a cellulose product made from tree pulp, processed in an environmentally friendly manner. Other man-made fibers are produced in a single, long filament, but are often cut into staple-like lengths before spinning to more closely resemble the properties of natural fibers.

Before the fibers are spun into yarn, they are combed or carded in order to align the fibers. At this point, they may be blended with other fibers. The fibers are then spun together into an S twist or a Z twist, depending on which way they are turned. The twisted strand, or ply, is

'S' twist & 'Z' twist

29

spun with one or more other plies in the opposite direction to make a multi-plied yarn. Plying fibers adds strength and balance to the yarn. Sometimes the plying step is omitted, however, resulting in a yarn made of one twisted strand, known as singles.

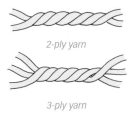

2-ply yarn

3-ply yarn

Most commercial yarns are spun by machine, but you may also be able to find some lovely handspun yarns. Dyeing may take place at any part of the process — before the yarn is processed (referred to as dyed in the fleece), as carded/combed fibers, or as finished yarn.

. . . .

Q **What are the characteristics of wool that make it so very popular?**

A Wool is warm, insulating, resilient, breathable, water-repellent, dirt-resistant, and naturally flame retardant, and it takes dye well. Different breeds of sheep yield wool with different characteristics. It is weaker wet than dry, but it can absorb up to 30% of its weight in moisture without feeling wet. It may felt if subjected to heat, moisture, and friction. Some manufacturers make wool machine washable by treating it to the "superwash" process.

. . . .

Q **What are the best-known characteristics of cotton?**

A Cotton is inelastic, heavy, absorbent, non-insulating, and takes dye well. It has a tendency to stretch, although it may also shrink when washed. It is usually machine washable and is stronger wet than dry.

....

Q **What makes mohair so appealing?**

A Mohair is durable, resilient, strong, and soil-resistant. It accepts dye well and is very warm for its weight. The staples are long and lustrous.

....

Q **What are the characteristics that make synthetics so useful?**

A The range of synthetic fibers is so vast that it is necessary to generalize. Manufacturers continually attempt to make synthetic yarns that mimic the best properties of the natural fibers. Synthetics are usually durable, water-resistant, strong, non-breathable, non-wicking, and non-insulating. Many synthetics are machine washable. Most are very sensitive to heat, and melt or burn at fairly low temperatures. Synthetics are well-suited for the many currently popular novelty yarns.

....

Q What is the difference between yarn and thread?

A Crocheters use both terms, sometimes interchangeably. Thread is generally thinner, and made from cotton, silk, or linen. It is often used for bedspreads, doilies, and lace. Yarn is everything else! In this book, I use the word "yarn" for both, unless otherwise stated.

Yarn Facts and Figures

Q How is yarn size described?

A For years, publishers and yarn manufacturers have attempted to come up with meaningful classifications for the size of yarns, and knitters and crocheters have attempted to pigeonhole yarns into these classifications.

Most recently, weight has been the determining factor, but we must be careful with the term *weight*, because it is used in this case to mean thickness, or the yarn's diameter. (Yarn diameter is also called *grist*.) In reality, how much a yarn actually weighs is less meaningful than its diameter and loft. The diameter of the yarn is one of the most important words we can use in effectively describing yarns, yet we still call it weight. Some yarns like brushed mohair, however, have a relatively small diameter compared to its loft — the amount of air between the fibers, or the amount of space the yarn occupies.

In other words, the fuzzy bits of the mohair make it a heavier "weight" yarn than it would be without fuzziness.

The table on the following pages gives the generally accepted yarn types in the United States. In the United Kingdom and other countries, the same names may refer to different sized yarns, or you may run into different terms altogether.

Q How is thread size described?

A Thread is generally described in numbers ranging from a superfine, truly threadlike size 100 to a more yarn-like size 3. The higher the number, the smaller the diameter of the thread. Thread may also be categorized by the number of plies. Some threads are more tightly spun than others. Many cotton yarns are mercerized or subjected to a chemical treatment that adds strength and luster.

Q How is yarn packaged?

A Yarn is sold in put-ups of skeins, balls, or loose hanks (also called skeins). A hank (or skein) of yarn is loosely wound, usually from a reel or swift, then tied in several places. You must wind it into a ball before working with it. Balls and commercially wound skeins are neatly wound packages that you can use immediately. The weight of the put-up varies, but is commonly 1.75 oz (50 g) or 3.5 oz (100 g). You may find synthetic yarns put up in larger quantities.

Yarn Weights
with Recommended Hook Sizes and Gauges

YARN WEIGHT	TYPES OF YARN
THREAD	Crochet cotton, bedspread cotton
1 SUPER FINE	Sock, fingering, baby
2 FINE	Sport, baby
3 LIGHT	DK, light worsted
4 MEDIUM	Worsted, afghan, aran
5 BULKY	Chunky, craft, rug
6 SUPER BULKY	Bulky, roving

Adapted from: Standards & Guidelines for Crochet and Knitting, by the Craft Yarn Council of America, www.yarnstandards.com

RECOMMENDED HOOK SIZE IN METRIC (US) TERMS	RECOMMENDED GAUGE IN SINGLE CROCHET, OVER 4" (10 MM)
Steel hooks 1.75 mm and smaller	
2.25–3.5 mm (B/1 to E/4)	21–32 sts
3.5–4.5 mm (E/4 to 7)	16–20 sts
4.5–5.5 mm (7 to I/9)	12–17 sts
5.5–6.5 mm (I/9 to K/10.5)	11–14 sts
6.5–10.5 mm K/10.5 to M/13)	8–11 sts
9 mm (M/13 and larger)	5–9 sts

Q What information can I find on the yarn band?

A Whether packaged in skeins, balls, or hanks, most yarn or thread is labeled with information on the fiber content; suggested gauge; weight and/or yardage of the skein, ball, or hank; laundering instructions; dye lot; color number; and possibly a color name. Suggested crochet hook and knitting needle sizes and gauge are also often included.

· ·

Q What do all those symbols on the yarn band mean?

A These are international symbols that provide the information described in the previous answer, even if you can't read the language on the band. The symbols are especially helpful if you purchased an imported yarn. Information on the suggested gauge and hook/needle sizes may also be shown in graphic form.

SEE ALSO: *Page 300, for more on yarn care symbols.*

| **WASH AT** **104°F/40°C** | **TUMBLE** **DRY** | **DO NOT** **TUMBLE DRY** | **DRY** **CLEAN** |

Q **What is a dye lot?**

A Yarns are dyed together in large batches or dye lots of the same color. Each dye lot is numbered, so you can tell if two skeins of yarn were dyed at the same time in the same batch. There can be subtle or not-so-subtle differences between dye lots.

. . . .

Q **Does dye lot really matter?**

A Many times it matters a great deal. Even if the dye lot differences are not apparent in the packaged ball or skein, they often show up in the finished project. Whether it matters on your project depends on how close together you use same-color yarns of different dye lots in the garment. If they are adjacent, you probably shouldn't mix them, as even subtle dye lot differences show. However, if the yarns are separated by another color, it is probably safe to mix dye lots in the same item.

When purchasing yarn for a project, your best bet is to be sure that all of the same-color yarn comes from the same dye lot.

. . . .

Q How do I know if the yarn colors I've chosen will look good together?

A In the store, hold them together and squint. Try to do this in daylight, not under fluorescent lighting. At home, wrap each of the colors around a white index card side by side, in the same proportions that you will use them in the finished project. Look at the card critically. Are the colors pleasing together or is one of them jarring? Can you put them next to each other in any order? Is there one that shouldn't be adjacent to another? If you are satisfied with the results on the index card, try all the colors together in a swatch.

SEE ALSO: *Pages 124–25, for swatching.*

Q I found the perfect color, but my yarn store doesn't have enough skeins from the same dye lot to complete my project. Do I ever dare use different dye lots in the same project?

A Try some of these ideas for minimizing problems when using different dye lots:

▶ Separate the different dye lots with a stripe of a different color.

▶ Switch stitch patterns where the dye lots change. Often a difference in texture can hide a slight color change.

▶ Make the odd dye lot a separate element, such as a pocket, collar, or border.

▶ Work a chain stitch or other surface embellishment over the spot where the dye lots meet.

....

Q **Why are some yarns labeled "No Dye Lot"?**

A These are synthetic (man-made) yarns. The chemical process allows producers to get exactly the same color results every time they produce a fiber in a particular color.

═══════════════════════════════════════

Yarn Substitutions

Q **Can I use a different yarn than the pattern calls for?**

A Yes, but you'll need to use a yarn similar to the one the pattern calls for to get similar results.

....

Q **How do I find a substitute yarn?**

A Start by noting what you know about the original yarn. What weight is it? What gauge does the pattern call for? What is the suggested hook size?

Next, look at the yarn you'd like to substitute and make sure it is the same weight as the original yarn. (Remember, I'm not referring to how much it weighs, but rather the weight classification.) The yarn band gives you the suggested gauge and hook size for the new yarn.

You may also want to consider other characteristics of the original yarn. What is the fiber content? Is it a plain yarn? Fuzzy? Smooth? Fluffy? Stiff? Tightly or loosely spun? A loosely spun yarn or a singles yarn will look different from a yarn with a tighter twist, even if they are the same weight. If you are not able to determine these characteristics from the description in the pattern, you may have to infer the information from a picture. These are just some characteristics to consider, however. You may not mind if the substitute yarn is not exactly the same as the original.

Because of their unique properties, novelty yarns may be tricky to substitute in a pattern. If you are unsure, check with a knowledgeable sales clerk where you buy your yarn.

. . . .

My pattern calls for 3-ply wool. Will any 3-ply wool be sufficient?

Not necessarily. In the past, yarns were often categorized according to the number of plies. This worked because there were a limited number of commercially available yarns, and everyone understood a 3-ply yarn to be of a certain diameter. These days, it is not sufficient to describe yarns by ply alone, as some multi-ply yarns are very fine and some singles are ultra bulky. You'll need to determine the weight classification of the original yarn and choose an appropriate substitute.

SEE ALSO: *Page 34 for yarn weight classifications.*

Q Can I buy yarn by weight?

A If you're referring to its weight classification, then the answer is, "yes." If you mean you want to figure the amount of yarn you need to buy based on how much each skein weighs, then the answer is, "bad idea." Buying by skein weight is another holdover from the past, when most yarns were wool and of a fairly uniform size. Length (yardage) is what matters, not how much the yarn weighs. Cotton yarn weighs more per yard than wool; some wools weigh more per yard than others. If yardage is not listed on the ball band, see if you can determine it from other sources so that you buy yarn for your project.

Q Can I use two lighter weight yarns together to make a heavier yarn?

A Yes, but you'll have to work a gauge swatch to see if you can get the correct gauge. To get off on the right foot, try using this rule of thumb: Add the suggested gauge of each of the two yarns and divide by 3 for the suggested gauge of the two yarns held together.

For example: Using two strands of sport-weight yarn with a suggested gauge of 4 sc = 1" (2.5 cm), double the gauge of the yarn and divide by 3:

$$(4 \times 2) \div 3 = 2.67 \text{ sc} = 1"$$

If the gauge you are expecting to use is in the ballpark of 2.5 sc = 1", then you might be able to use those two strands of sport-weight yarn together. Don't forget that you'll need a larger hook than you would for a single strand of sport-weight yarn. You'll probably start with the hook size listed in the pattern instructions. Swatch with your proposed yarn and hook to see how close you are. If you are using a yarn doubled, remember that you'll also have to double the amount of yardage called for in the pattern!

SEE ALSO: *Pages 124–25, for swatching.*

Q If I'm substituting yarn, how much do I buy?

A Figure out how much yardage you need by multiplying the number of skeins the pattern calls for by the number of yards per skein of the original yarn. You should be able to find this information in the pattern instructions. Once you know the total yardage you need for your project, divide that number by the number of yards per skein in the yarn you want to use. You'll probably get a fraction. Be sure to round up since you cannot buy a fraction of a ball of yarn.

For example: My pattern calls for 8 skeins of Pretty Yarn (100% acrylic, 200 yds/100 g). I want to use Beautiful Yarn (100% wool, 150 yds/100 g) instead. Here's the math:

$$8 \text{ skeins} \times 200 \text{ yards} = 1600 \text{ yards}$$
$$1600 \text{ yards} \div 150 \text{ yards} = \text{about } 11 \text{ balls}$$

You may want to buy one additional ball for safety's sake. Remember, you'll be using up yarn making a good-sized swatch.

Be sure you are using consistent units of measure (yards or meters). If one yarn is labeled in meters and one in yards, you'll need to convert the yards to meters or vice versa before calculating how much yarn you need.

. . . .

Q **Do you have any advice on how to calculate yarn amounts when I'm designing my own garments?**

A That's the 6 million dollar question, isn't it? The amount of yarn you need depends on the size of the yarn, the stitch pattern, your gauge, and the size of the item you are making. When you follow a published pattern, the instructions are your guide. Many people buy an extra ball of yarn, just to be certain to have enough. You can always use leftover yarn for another project, and many stores accept returns of extra balls for credit. If you don't have a pattern to go by, find a published pattern for an item similar to your design, using a yarn of similar weight, and estimate your needs.

You can also estimate your yarn needs when you make your swatch. Before you begin the swatch, pull out a length of yarn (say, 5 or 10 yards), jot down the measurement, and tie a loose overhand knot. If you reach the knot before completing your swatch, untie the knot, reel out more yarn, jot down the new measurement, and tie another loose knot. When the swatch is complete, measure how much yarn is left before you get to the knot. Subtract this amount from the total of the yardage that you pulled out of the ball. This is the total yardage you used for the swatch, including yarn tails. Now, measure the area of your swatch in square inches.

For example: Number of yards used for swatch ÷ square inches in swatch = Number of yards used per square inch

Now, estimate the total area of your project in square inches. It's easy if your project is a square or rectangle: Just multiply the width times the height. But if you're making a sweater, the calculation is a bit more complicated. Here's the formula:

(Total finished chest measurement × length of sweater) + (width of top of sleeve + width of sleeve cuff) × length of sleeve = Area of sweater

Total area of sweater × Number of yards used per square inch = Total number of inches needed for project

Remember — this is just an estimate!

When you finish a project, make a note of how much yarn you used so you can refer to it in the future.

. . . .

Q **How do I convert from yards to meters?**

A One meter equals 1.09 yards, so you need to divide the number of yards by 1.09 to get the conversion to meters. Another way to think of it is that a meter is about 10% longer than a yard.

For example: To convert 15 yards to meters:

$$15 \div 1.09 = 13.76 \text{ meters}$$

. . . .

Q **How do I convert from meters to yards?**

A Reverse the process and multiply the number of meters by 1.09.

For example: To convert 25 meters to yards:

$$25 \times 1.09 = 27.25 \text{ yards}$$

. . . .

Q **My pattern calls for a yarn that has been discontinued. Is there any way to find out about the characteristics of discontinued yarns to help me choose an appropriate substitute?**

A   There are resources available to help you find out more about yarns, even those that are discontinued. Local yarn shop owners often have information on discontinued yarns, and really experienced ones may even be able to play "Name That Yarn" with just a glance.

You can also search the Internet. Sellers on eBay often offer older yarn, complete with fiber and yardage information. Try Google (or other search engines) for the yarn name and manufacturer. As of the time of this writing, www.wise-needle.com and other sites have complete information and reviews on yarns, both current and discontinued. You might also try contacting the yarn company itself; again, you can find address information on the Internet or in crochet and knitting magazines.

Working with Yarns

Q **What is the best way to pull yarn from the ball?**

A Usually pulling from the center is best. If you are using a commercially packaged skein or ball, first look to see if the outside strand of the yarn is tucked into the center of the ball.

commercially wound ball

If it is, pull it out but don't use it. Stick your fingers into the center of the ball and fish around to see if you can find the inner end. You may need to pull out a little wad of yarn in order to find the tail. This is the end to use.

Note: If you are working with the yarn doubled, you may use both the end from the center and the one from the outside of the ball.

. . . .

Q **How do I handle an unwound hank of yarn?**

A Don't try to work directly from the hank or you'll be sorry! You need to wind it into a ball before you start stitching. You can use a yarn swift, lampshade, chair, or someone willing to hold the yarn for you. Untwist the hank and hang it carefully on your holder — animate or inanimate. If the yarn is tied in several places, cut the shorter pieces of yarn and throw them away. Sometimes there is a single knot where the beginning and end meet, wrapped in such a way as to keep the yarn from tangling. Be especially watchful in the beginning, because you may have to unwrap the yarn from around the skein for the first few feet. Cut the knot and take a single end in your hand, winding carefully for the first round or two until you are certain that the yarn is unwinding without tangling.

SEE ALSO: *Pages 23–24, for more on ball winders and swifts.*

. . . .

Q Can I create my own center-pull ball?

A Yes. The easiest way is with a ball winder, which winds the skein into a nice center-pull form. If you don't have a ball winder, however, you can do it manually:

1. Hold the starting end between your thumb and forefinger and spread your other fingers. Keeping the tail secure with your thumb, wind the yarn in a figure eight around your fingers about a dozen times. Don't let the strands overlap each other.

2. Pinching the yarn where it crosses itself, slide the yarn off your fingers.

3. Fold the bundle of yarn in half.

4. Keeping 10–12 inches (25–30 cm) of the tail end dangling, start winding the yarn loosely around

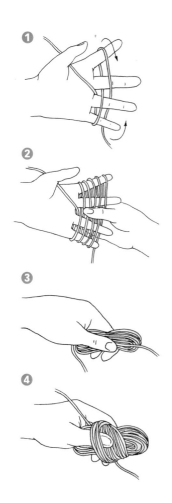

this little wad of yarn, turning it this way and that to form a ball. Wrap the yarn over your fingers to ensure that you are wrapping loosely enough. When you have finished winding, you should be able to pull on the tail coming out of the middle of the ball.

. . . .

Q How do I know if my ball is wound too tightly?

A Your ball should not be hard — it should have a bit of spring to it. Yarn wound too tightly is stretched and tense, which is apt to cause trouble once it's made into a fabric. The yarn may become permanently stretched, decreasing its elasticity. Even if it isn't permanently ruined, if you stitch the yarn up in its stretched state and then wash it, it will return to its natural, un-stretched state, with possible undesirable consequences to the size of the piece! If you wind a center-pull ball, the ball collapses in on itself as it is used, releasing any extra tension.

. . . .

Q How can I keep my yarn from splitting?

A If your yarn splits, it may be that the yarn is not of high quality or that it is loosely spun. Some hooks with pointy tips may split the yarn. In that case, you may need to stitch extra carefully to avoid splitting the yarn, or use a different hook. A hook with a rough spot also sometimes splits the yarn. Try sanding the rough spot with very fine sandpaper. If that doesn't work, discard the hook.

If your yarn is coming untwisted as you work, examine how you are pulling it from the ball. If you are using a center-pull ball, you may be removing twist because of the direction you are pulling. Try pulling from the opposite side of the ball or using the end from the outside of the ball.

. . . .

Q **What should I do when I reach a knot in the yarn?**

A Even high-quality yarns may have a knot or a weak spot every now and then. Don't work over it. Instead, cut the yarn several inches before the knot, leaving a tail to be woven in later. Cut out the bad spot, then begin again, just as you would when adding a new ball.

SEE ALSO: *Page 54, for starting a new yarn.*

When you begin a new row, pull out enough yarn to work the entire row, so that you can see any imperfection before you reach it. You can then cut the yarn and rejoin it at the beginning of the row and thus avoid starting a new yarn in the middle of the fabric.

Working with Challenging Yarns

Q **What is a novelty yarn?**

A Just as its name implies, this isn't your run-of-the-mill yarn. You'll know it when you see it. The fun of a novelty yarn comes from its unique characteristics — it can be made from almost anything and spun in almost any way. It may have a great deal of texture, or it may be spun with non-fiber additives like beads or feathers. It may have little bits of stuff hanging from a main core. It may be a thin "crochet along" (or "knit along") thread meant to be held together with another strand of yarn as you stitch, or it may be as bulky as your thumb.

Novelty yarns are often described by their characteristics: eyelash, slub, metallic, ribbon, or bouclé (meaning curly in

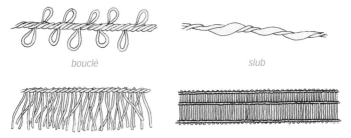

bouclé

slub

eyelash

ribbon

French). When substituting one novelty yarn for another, choose a similar yarn type in order to achieve a similar look.

 I've tried working with novelty yarns, but found them frustrating. Do you have any suggestions?

 Novelty yarns and fuzzy yarns are beautiful, but they can present a challenge for crocheters. Here are some tips that may make it easier if you are using a novelty yarn:

▶ Use your fingers as well as your eyes to determine where to put the hook.

▶ Work between stitches rather than into actual stitches. (If you are following written instructions, be aware that the gauge and look of the fabric will be different from fabric stitched in the standard way.)

working between stitches

▶ Work with a larger hook than you normally would use for the weight of your yarn. Again, pay attention to your gauge if you are following a printed pattern.

▶ Try a mesh stitch rather than a solid stitch pattern. It's easier to work into chain spaces than into stitches.

▶ Work two strands together — a smooth yarn along with the novelty yarn — to help distinguish the stitches.

SEE ALSO: Pages 87–90, for where to place the hook.

Q **Do you have tips for working with slippery yarn?**

Yarn Bra

A Rayon ribbons and other yarns are beautiful to look at, but they too present a challenge. Even if you wind them carefully, the balls have a tendency to melt into a puddle at the first opportunity. Try corralling them into a sandwich bag or wrap them with a Yarn Bra, old stocking, or other stretchy material for better control.

SEE ALSO: *Pages 55–56, for weaving in slippery ends.*

Q **Is there anything I can do to keep variegated yarns from appearing splotchy?**

A When you get noticeable odd-shaped areas of a single color in the middle of a piece of crochet, it's known as "pooling." Try alternating two balls of yarn or use the inside and outside ends of a single ball of yarn each row or round to avoid pooling. Or, use a stitch pattern that breaks up large expanses of the variegated yarn: spike stitches, contrasting color stripes, or texture stitches.

As the distance across the piece changes, the frequency with which certain colors show up changes. For instance, when you shape the armholes and neck edge, the distance the yarn travels is shorter, so the color repeats create a different pattern on these shorter rows than in the longer rows below.

Therefore, you may need to use these anti-pooling techniques on some parts of a garment and not on others. (Voice of Experience: You can't tell from a small swatch if your colors are going to pool.)

. . . .

Q **Is there any kind of yarn I can't crochet with?**

A Not that I've found, although some yarns may be more challenging than others.

Endings & Beginnings

Q **How do I add a new yarn?**

A It's best to start a new ball of yarn at the edge if you can. The technique is the same no matter which stitch you are working: Work until there are two loops left on the hook, yarn over with the new yarn and pull through both loops on hook.

If you don't already have a stitch on the hook, just insert the hook into the proper spot, yarn over and pull up a loop. Treat this loop as you would a slip

adding a new yarn mid-row

knot; you may need to chain for the height of your first stitch. Leave a tail at least 6" (15 cm) long on both the old and new yarns so that you can weave in the ends later.

SEE ALSO: *Page 73, for stitch heights.*

Q I hate weaving in ends. Is there any way to take care of tails left when starting a new color or ball so that I don't have to worry about them later?

A Many crocheters like to work over the tail of the old yarn as they work the first few stitches in a new yarn. As you begin a new yarn, hold the tails of yarn to the left along the top of the stitches on the previous row or round. When you insert the hook into the next stitch and pull up a loop, make sure that you are working around the tails, catching and securing them into the fabric as you work each of the next couple of inches of stitches. If you find that this method is too bulky, just catch one of the ends, or leave the ends to be woven in later.

Q I'm using a very slippery yarn and finding it partic- ularly difficult to hide the ends, which tend to pop out of the finished fabric. Do you have suggestions?

A The usual method of weaving in ends as you work is less successful with slippery yarns, and it also may not hide contrasting yarns satisfactorily. Some silk and rayon ribbons take any opportunity to slide free. Whenever you're working with these yarns, leave longer ends (8"/20 cm), so that when the fabric is finished, you can work them diagonally through the back of several stitches one way, and then diagonally in the opposite direction. You could also try tacking down the ends with sewing thread in a matching color. You may find it helpful to put a dot of soft fabric glue on the ends. (Try it first on your swatch to make sure you are happy with the way it feels against your skin.)

SEE ALSO: *Pages 235–37, for more on weaving in ends.*

CHAPTER 3

Strong Foundations

EVERY PIECE OF CROCHET has to start somewhere. The *foundation chain* serves as a base into which you work your first row of stitches. To make the foundation chain, begin with a slip knot on the hook.

Basic Foundation Chains

Q **How do I make a slip knot?**

A Begin by crossing the yarn over itself about 6" (15 cm) from the end to form a loop. The short end of the yarn is called the *tail*. Arrange the loop so that the yarn coming from the ball (the working yarn) is under the loop. Then proceed as follows:

1. Insert hook under the working yarn in the center of the loop.

2. Pull through another loop formed by the yarn still attached to the ball (the *working yarn*).

3. Tug gently on the working yarn to snug the knot around the hook.

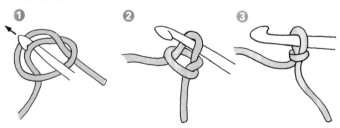

Q How do I make the foundation chain?

A Begin with a slip knot on the hook as described in the previous question, then proceed as follows:

1. Wrap the yarn around the hook from back to front and draw the working yarn through the slip knot.

2. Continue to wrap the yarn over the hook (this is called a *yarnover* [yo]) and to pull it through the loop (lp) on the hook (hk).

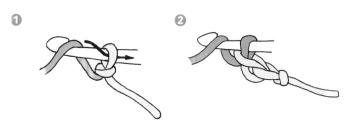

Q What should I do if I'm having trouble getting the loop on my hook over the head of the hook?

A The problem might be the slip knot: Make sure that your slip knot isn't too tight. If the problem is subsequent stitches, be sure that you aren't holding the yarn too tightly whenever you are making a stitch. The following technique may also help:

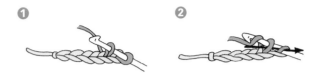

rotating the hook to draw the yarn through

1. When making the yarnover, the head of the hook should be facing you.

2. As you pull the yarn through the loop on the hook, rotate the hook head 90 degrees so that it faces down toward the chain.

. . . .

Q How do I keep the growing foundation chain under control?

A With the working yarn over your forefinger, hold the piece that you are stitching with your thumb and middle finger near the hook. As the chain gets longer, keep moving your fingers up close to the hook.

. . . .

Q How do I make an even chain?

A Chaining evenly takes a bit of practice. When you're just starting to learn to crochet, it may take a while

before you are comfortable holding the yarn and hook. Try not to be discouraged! Concentrate on working loosely and evenly, and practice keeping the fingers that are holding the yarn close to the hook. Make sure to form your stitches on the shank of the hook and not on the narrower throat.

SEE ALSO: *Page 12, for parts of the crochet hook.*

Q How will I know if my foundation chain is the correct tension?

A Do your stitches look consistent? All the stitches should look almost the same size. Were you easily able to work your first row into the chain? After you have worked the foundation chain and the first row or two of your piece, lay it flat on

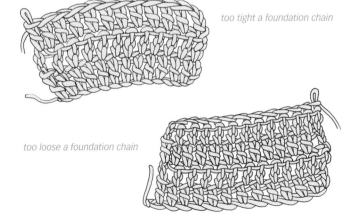

too tight a foundation chain

too loose a foundation chain

a table and look at it critically. Do the stitches in the next rows flare above the foundation chain? If so, you need a looser chain. Do the stitches pull in above the foundation? If so, you need a tighter foundation chain. In either case, start over from scratch to make the appropriate adjustments. (Voice of Experience: You'll save time and effort if you make these adjustments while you're still working on your sample swatch and not wait until the actual project.

SEE ALSO: *Pages 123–25, for swatches.*

Q How do I fix a foundation chain that's too tight?

A Unfortunately, there is no good fix for a too-tight foundation chain, so it's important to get it right from the beginning. If you notice right away that your chain is too tight, rip it out and start over. You may find it helps to use a larger hook for the foundation chain, and then switch on the first row or round to the size you need to get the correct gauge.

SEE ALSO: *Pages 122–23 for gauge.*

Q How do I count chains?

A This question confounds many crocheters. Hold your chain so that it is not twisted; you should see a stack of V's facing you. Count each V as a stitch, but don't count the slip knot or the loop on the hook.

counting the chain

Some crocheters find that it makes counting easier if they insert a marker every 10 or 20 stitches when making a long chain.

markers in foundation chain

It's also a good idea to chain a few too many when working a long chain. That way, if you missed your count by a few stitches, you don't have to start over! You can pick out any extra chains later.

picking out extra chains

. . . .

 How long does my foundation chain have to be?

If you are following a published pattern, the instructions tell you. Sometimes the instructions say to work a "multiple of 4 plus 2." This means that your stitch pattern requires any multiple of 4 stitches, plus 2 for turning or to balance a stitch pattern (for instance, 6, 10, 14, or more chains).

SEE ALSO: *Page 117, for multiples.*

If you are working without a published pattern, chain as many stitches as you need for the number of stitches you want on the first row, plus the number you need for a turning chain. The number of stitches in a turning chain is based on the height of the first stitch you'll work on the first row.

SEE ALSO: *Page 73, for height of stitches.*

 Where in the stitch do I insert my hook into a foundation chain?

Take a moment to look at the construction of the chain. The front of the chain looks like a row of sideways V's; the back of the chain has a row of bumps. On the first row, insert your hook under both the top loop of the V and the bump. Sometimes this is described as the "top 2 loops" of the chain. However, if your yarn makes this difficult, or if you are unhappy with the way your first row looks, try

front of chain   *back of chain*

inserting the hook into just the top loop of the chain. Just be sure to be consistent across the row.

Starting the First Row

FIRST STITCH OF FIRST ROW	EXTRA STITCHES IN FOUNDATION CHAIN	CHAINS FROM HOOK FOR FIRST STITCH
Slip stitch	1	2nd
Single crochet	1	2nd
Half double crochet	2	3rd
Double crochet	3	4th
Triple/Treble crochet	4	5th

SEE ALSO: *Pages 74–75, for single, double, half double, triple crochet, and slip stitch.*

Q Which of the stitches in the foundation chain should I start with?

A Which stitch you insert the hook into first depends on what type of stitch you are working on the first row. The taller the stitch, the further back along the chain you insert the hook. When the first stitch after the foundation chain is going to be single crochet, insert the hook into the second chain from the hook. Consult the table above for other stitches.

Q Does it really matter which way I wrap the yarn over the hook?

A Yes, always wrap the yarn over the hook from back to front.

....

Q How can I tell if my foundation chain is twisted?

A The chain should look like a little row of stacked V's from the front side. If it doesn't, you twisted your chain. Rip back to the place where it was twisted and rework.

Variations on Foundation Chains

Q Do I always have to work a foundation chain?

A Not always. Although you always need some sort of base into which to work the first row or round of stitches, there is an option other than a foundation chain. You can combine the foundation chain and first row of the stitching into a single step. These chainless foundations create an elastic edge and may prevent a too-tight foundation chain. They are often used in place of a chain and a single row of stitches, as for a cord, or for increasing many stitches at the edge of a piece. However, because they do not look exactly like a standard "foundation chain plus Row 1," the two methods should probably not be mixed within the same project. Here's how to make both single and double crochet foundations:

MAKING A SINGLE CROCHET FOUNDATION

1. Make a slip knot on the hook and chain 2.

2. Work a single crochet into the second chain from hook.

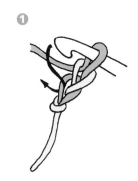

3. Insert hook into left-most loop of stitch just made, and work single crochet into this stitch.

Continue to work a single crochet stitch into the left-most loop of the stitch just made, until the desired number of stitches is reached.

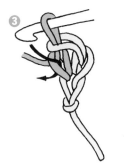

MAKING A DOUBLE CROCHET FOUNDATION

1. Make a slip knot on the hook and chain 3.

2. Work a double crochet into the third chain from hook.

3. Yarn over and insert hook into bottom left-most loop of stitch just made.

4. Work double crochet into this stitch. Continue to work a double crochet stitch into the bottom left-most loop of the stitch just made, until the desired number of stitches is reached.

....

Q My instructions say to "work on opposite side of chain." What does that mean?

A Sometimes you need to stitch into both sides of the foundation chain, for instance, when you are making an oval or starting a three-dimensional piece. Typically, you start by working a row into the foundation chain in the usual way, inserting your hook into the top loop or top two loops as described earlier. If you want a rounded end, work several stitches into the last stitch of the foundation chain, then rotate the chain so that the front side is still facing you but the bottom of the chain is now on top. Continue to work stitches into the remaining unworked loops on the other side of chain, placing several stitches into the last stitch to match the other end. Join with a slip stitch to the first stitch.

SEE ALSO: *Pages 146–47, for stitching an oval.*

If you want a square end rather than a rounded end, cut the yarn and end off after working the first row across the foundation chain. Turn the piece so that the row you just worked is on the bottom and the remaining loops of the foundation chain are on top. With right side facing, rejoin the yarn at the right-hand corner and stitch into each loop on the other side of the chain. You also work into the opposite side of the chain when you add on edging.

SEE ALSO: *Page 218, for edgings.*

Q How can I get the beginning and ending rows of my piece to look the same?

A When you work the first row, if you insert your hook into just the bumps of the chain instead of into both the top loop and the bump, the beginning and ending rows will look the same.

CHAPTER 4

In Stitches

THE WORD *stitch* in crochet sometimes refers to the most familiar stitch patterns, such as slip stitch and single crochet, or it may be used to indicate variations of the basics like popcorn and shells. In this chapter, we'll talk about all of these.

The Basic Stitches

Q How are stitches formed?

A At its most basic, crochet is just a series of loops. Every crochet stitch pattern, no matter how complex, is made up of only three basic movements, all involving loops:

1. Wrap yarn around hook (yarn over).
2. Insert hook somewhere.
3. Pull yarn through something.

The combination of these three steps, the order in which they are accomplished, and the placement of the hook makes for the endless variety of crocheted stitch patterns available to us.

Q What is a *stitch pattern*?

A A stitch pattern is a specific combination of stitches that, when repeated, creates a crocheted fabric. Sometimes just the word *stitch* is used as a shortcut for the phrase.

Q What are the most common stitches?

A The most familiar stitch patterns are single crochet (sc) and double crochet (dc). Slip stitch (sl st), half double crochet (hdc), and treble crochet (tr) are also commonly used, even in simple designs.

· ·

Q How do I make the most common stitches?

A As mentioned, all crochet stitches are made using a similar series of movements. The shorter stitches require fewer steps than the taller stitches. On the following pages, you can find step-by-step illustrations of how to make each stitch. When you need at-a-glance information, go to the table on the next page for a quick reference (as well as a comparison) of what's involved for each stitch.

· ·

Q What does *stitch height* mean?

A With the exception of slip stitch, all crocheted stitches have height, ranging from the short single crochet, up to and beyond the tall treble crochet. Becoming familiar with the relative height of each stitch pattern helps you understand how long each turning chain must be. It is also useful when shaping curves in a piece.

Stitches at a Glance

	STEP 1	STEP 2	STEP 3
CHAIN STITCH	Yarn round hook	Pull yarn through stitch on hook	
SLIP STITCH	Insert hook into next stitch	Yarn round hook	Pull yarn through both loops on hook
SINGLE CROCHET	Insert hook into next stitch	Yarn round hook	Pull yarn through stitch (2 loops on hook)
HALF-DOUBLE CROCHET	Yarn round hook	Insert hook into next stitch	Pull yarn through stitch (3 loops on hook)
DOUBLE CROCHET	Yarn round hook	Insert hook into next stitch	Pull yarn through stitch (3 loops on hook)
TREBLE (TRIPLE) CROCHET	Yarn round hook twice	Insert hook into next stitch	Pull yarn through stitch (4 loops on hook)

SEE ALSO: *Pages 282–86, for stitch symbols*

STEP 4	STEP 5	STEPS 6–7	STEPS 8–9
Yarn round hook	Pull yarn through both loops on hook		
Yarn round hook	Pull yarn through 3 loops on hook		
Yarn round hook	Pull yarn through 2 loops on hook	Repeat Steps 4 and 5	
Yarn round hook	Pull yarn through 2 loops on hook	Repeat Steps 4 and 5	Repeat Steps 4 and 5

Q What are the stitches in order of height?

A The basic stitch patterns, in order of height are:

> Slip stitch
> Single crochet
> Half double crochet
> Double crochet
> Treble crochet

There are also some extended stitches that fall in between the basic stitches height-wise. The complete list is:

> Slip stitch
> Single crochet
> Extended single crochet
> Half double crochet
> Extended half double crochet
> Double crochet
> Extended double crochet
> Treble crochet
> Extended treble crochet
> Double treble crochet, and so on

. . . .

Q How do I make a single crochet stitch?

A The illustrations on pages 77–78 show how to make a single crochet into a chain and into a foundation row.

SINGLE CROCHET INTO A CHAIN

1. Insert the hook into the second chain from the hook, wrap the yarn over the hook (called *yarnover,* and abbreviated *yo*). Pull through a loop.

2. Now you have two loops on your hook.

3. Wrap the yarn over the hook again and pull it through both loops on the hook.

4. You've made one single crochet.

5. Continue working into the foundation chain all the way back to the slip knot, but don't work into the slip knot. Count to make sure you have the number of stitches you are supposed to have.

SINGLE CROCHET INTO AN ESTABLISHED ROW

1. Chain 1 to make a turning chain and get your hook up to the level of the single crochet stitch.

2. Turn the crochet counterclockwise so that you can work the next row from right to left (left to right for Lefties). Insert hook under both loops at the top of the last stitch in the previous row. (This is the stitch below the chain-1.)

3. Yarn over and pull up a loop, yarn over and pull through two loops (as in steps 1–4 for single crochet above). Continue across the row, working into both loops of each stitch across.

4. Be sure to work into the last stitch, then count again to make sure you still have the same number of stitches.

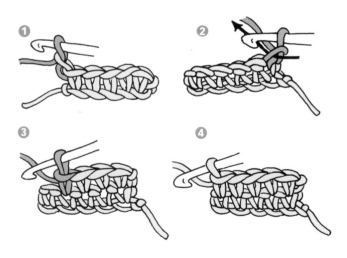

Q **How do I make a half double crochet stitch?**

A The steps below show how to make a half double crochet into a chain, as well as into an already-established foundation row.

HALF DOUBLE CROCHET INTO A CHAIN

1. Wrap the yarn over the hook, then insert the hook into the third chain from the hook.

2. Yarn over and pull through a loop. You have three loops on your hook.

3. Wrap the yarn over the hook again and pull it through all three loops on the hook.

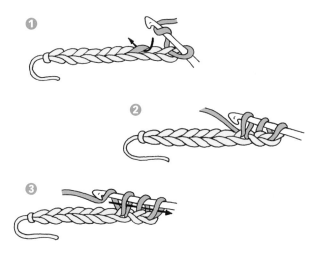

4. You've made one half double crochet.

5. Continue working into the foundation chain all the way back to the slip knot, but don't work into the slip knot. Count to make sure you have the number of stitches you are supposed to have. Count the two chains you skipped at the beginning of the row as a stitch.

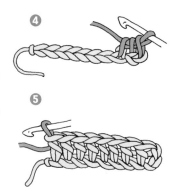

HALF DOUBLE CROCHET INTO AN ESTABLISHED ROW

1. Chain 2 to make a turning chain and get your hook up to the level of the half double crochet stitch. Turn the crochet counterclockwise so that you can work the next row from right to left (left to right for Lefties). Yarn over and insert hook under both loops at the top of the next-to-last stitch in the previous row.

2. Yarn over and pull up a loop, yarn over and pull

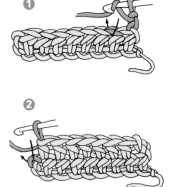

through all three loops (as in steps 2 and 3 for half double crochet above). Continue across the row, working into both loops of each stitch across. Work the last stitch into the top of the chain-2 turning chain from the previous row.

3. Count again to make sure you still have the same number of stitches, counting the beginning chain-2 as a stitch. Chain 2 to make a turning chain.

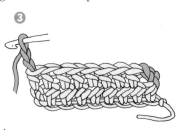

Q How do I make a double crochet stitch?

A The steps below show how to make a double crochet into a chain as well as into an already-established foundation row.

DOUBLE CROCHET INTO A CHAIN

1. Wrap the yarn over the hook, then insert the hook into the fourth chain from the hook.

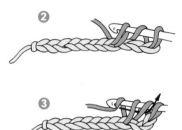

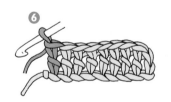

2. Yarn over and pull through a loop. You have three loops on your hook.

3. Wrap the yarn over the hook again and pull it through the first two loops on the hook.

4. You now have two loops on your hook.

5. Yarn over again and pull through both loops.

6. You've made one double crochet.

7. Continue working into the foundation chain all the way back to the slip knot, but don't work into the slip knot. Count to make sure you have the number of stitches you are supposed to have. Count the three chains you skipped at the beginning of the row as a stitch.

DOUBLE CROCHET INTO AN ESTABLISHED ROW

1. Chain 3 to make a turning chain and get your hook up to the level of the double crochet stitch. Turn the crochet counterclockwise so that you can work the next row from right to left (left to right for Lefties).

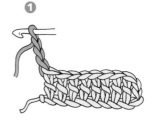

2. Yarn over and insert hook under both loops at the top of the next-to-last stitch in the previous row.

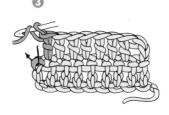

3. Yarn over and pull up a loop, yarn over and pull through two loops, then yarn over and pull through the remaining two loops (as in steps 2–5 for double crochets above). Continue across the row, working into both loops of each stitch across. Work the last stitch into the top of the chain-3 turning chain

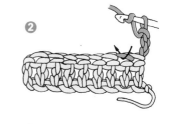

from the previous row. Count again to make sure you still have the same number of stitches, counting the beginning chain-3 as a stitch.

Q How do I make a triple crochet stitch?

A The steps below show how to make a triple crochet into a chain as well as into an already-established foundation row.

TRIPLE CROCHET INTO A CHAIN

1. Wrap the yarn over the hook two times, then insert the hook into the fifth chain from the hook.

2. Yarn over and pull through a loop.

3. You have four loops on your hook.

4. Yarn over and pull through the first two loops on the hook, leaving three loops on the hook.

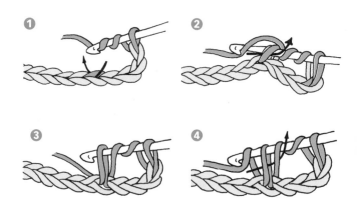

5. Yarn over again and pull through two loops.

6. You now have two loops on the hook.

7. One more "yarn over and pull through two loops" leaves you with a single loop on the hook and a completed triple crochet.

8. Continue working into the foundation chain all the way back to the slip knot, but don't work into the slip knot. Count to make sure you have the number of stitches you are supposed to have. Count the four chains you skipped at the beginning of the row as a stitch.

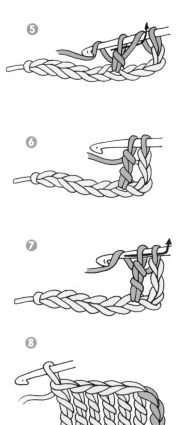

TRIPLE CROCHET INTO AN ESTABLISHED ROW

1. Chain 4 to make a turning chain and get your hook up to the level of the triple crochet stitch. Turn the crochet counterclockwise so that you can work the next row from right to left (left to right for Lefties).

2. Yarn over twice and insert hook under both loops at the top of the next-to-last stitch in the previous row.

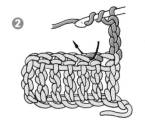

3. Continue with the triple crochet stitch (as described in steps 2–7, above). Work the last stitch into the top of the chain-4 turning chain from the previous row. Count again to make sure you still have the same number of stitches, counting the beginning chain-4 as a stitch.

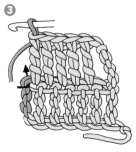

Placing the Hook and Turning Chains

Q Why did I work into the last stitch on the previous row for single crochet, but the next-to-last stitch on the previous row for the other stitches?

A In single crochet, the chain-1 turning chain does not count as a stitch, so you had to work a stitch into that same spot. In half double crochet and taller stitches, you do count the turning chain as a stitch. If you worked your first real stitch into the same stitch as the chain, you would be increasing a stitch, so you work the first stitch into the second stitch (the next-to-last stitch from the previous row).

Q What is a *turning chain?*

A A turning chain is the little chain worked at the beginning of a row to bring the hook up to the level of the stitches to be formed on the next row. Some patterns include the turning chain at the end of a row; others have it at the beginning of a row. Either method accomplishes the same goal.

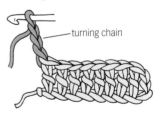

turning chain

Where do I insert my hook into a stitch at the begin- ning of a row?

The answer depends on whether you are counting a turning chain as a stitch. If the turning chain at the beginning of the row is not going to count as a stitch, insert the hook into the base of the turning chain. If the turning chain is going to count as a stitch, skip the base of the turning chain and insert the hook into the first sideways V that you see.

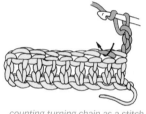 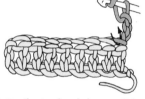

counting turning chain as a stitch   *not counting turning chain as a stitch*

 What does it mean to "insert hook into next stitch"?

The top of each stitch looks like a sideways V or chain. When you work back and forth in rows, the V lies slightly to the left of the next stitch that you made in the previous row. When you work in rounds, the V lies slightly to the right of the next stitch that you made in the previous round. Insert the hook into both legs of this V unless your pattern instructions say otherwise.

Q **How do I know if the turning chain should be counted as a stitch?**

A If you are following a published pattern, the instructions should tell you. For example, the second row of the pattern might read:

Row 2: Ch 3 (counts as dc), dc in each dc to end.

The "counts as dc" means that this chain-3 turning chain (abbreviated *ch-3*) is meant to be counted as a stitch, so you should work into the top of it on the next row as if it were a regular double crochet. Subsequent pattern rows may not state "counts as dc" but you are meant to assume that all ch-3 turning chains count as a double crochet for this pattern unless the instructions say otherwise.

If you are designing your own pattern, you may choose whether or not to regard the turning chain as a stitch. Most of the time, in half double crochet and taller stitches, you do count the turning chain as a stitch. Some stitch patterns are easier to work if the turning chain is not part of the pattern.

Single crochet turning chains are short and often hard to find or work into, so you may decide to use the ch-1 turning chain as an "extra" stitch.

No matter which method you use — counting a turning chain as a stitch or not — you should be consistent within your project. If you aren't consistent, you'll have difficulty maintaining the correct number of stitches across the row, resulting in uneven edges.

Q How do I know whether or not to work a stitch into the turning chain from the previous row?

A If a turning chain counts as a stitch on one row, you work a stitch into it on the next row.

· ·

Q How can I recognize a turning chain?

A It won't look quite like the other stitches. In fact, it may be a bit tricky to recognize where the "top" of the turning chain is. You may find it easier to locate the top of the turning chain if you first work the chain, then take the hook out and insert it from the other direction, instead of twisting the chain. Or you might find it helpful to put a stitch marker in the last chain of your turning chain, so that you can then work into the marked stitch on the return row.)

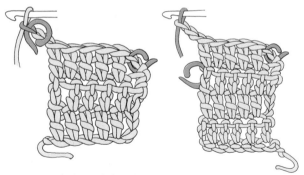

placing a stitch marker in last chain of turning chain

Working with the Stitches

Q **What does it mean when the directions say to "sc into each sc" or "dc into each sc"?**

A This is just a reminder of the nature of the stitch pattern in the previous row, combined with instruction about what stitch pattern was used in the current row. Knowing that you are making a single crochet row over a previous row of single crochet (in the first instance) or a row of double crochet over a row of single crochet (in the second instance) assures you that you are working the stitch pattern as intended.

SEE ALSO: *Page 164, for more on fabric.*

Q **My stitches don't look like the ones in the picture. Why not?**

A There are several possibilities for this:

▶ You may be having a problem with American/British terms. If you are reading a British pattern, you'll have to "translate" the pattern into American stitches to achieve the right look.

▶ Sometimes you must work several rows before you can see a stitch pattern develop. Stitch patterns with multiple row repeats may require a complete repeat or two before the pattern is apparent.

▶ Re-check the pattern instructions to see if there are any special instructions you missed. If you think you are following the instructions correctly, it may pay to continue for another few rows to see what develops.

. . . .

 Q **What's the difference between American and British pattern instructions?**

A Whoever said that the United States and the UK are two countries divided by a single language might have been thinking of crocheters, because crochet terminology differs significantly between the two countries. We use American terms throughout this book, but you need to be aware of the differences when reading a British pattern.

One Language, Two Meanings

US TERM	UK TERM
Single crochet	Double crochet
Half double crochet	Half treble
Double crochet	Treble
Triple/Treble crochet	Double treble
Double treble crochet	Triple/treble treble
Slip stitch	Single crochet

Q What is the difference between *triple crochet* and *treble crochet?*

A The way they are spelled! They are the same thing.

. . . .

Q What are some uses for slip stitch?

A The slip stitch is intended for joining rounds, for seaming, and for moving the yarn and hook to a different spot without adding height to a row. For example, when you are decreasing for an armhole, you might use slip stitch to move the yarn and hook in from the edge of the fabric without building height.

SEE ALSO: *Page 101, for slip stitch.*

Q What are some uses for chain stitch?

A The versatile chain stitch is ideal for shoelaces, ties, drawstrings, handles, buttonholes, turning chains, foundation chains, decorative increases, and lacy stitch patterns.

. . . .

Q What does it mean to "pull up a loop"?

A This is the basic move in every crochet stitch. It means to wrap the yarn around the hook and pull it through the fabric. It is usually preceded by "insert hook into stitch/fabric/etc. and . . .."

. . . .

Q Do I have to put my hook into the top of the next stitch as I crochet?

A Certainly not! Exploring new territory with your hook makes crochet endlessly intriguing. There are many places you can put your hook other than into the "next stitch." Once you're familiar with the basic stitch patterns, you can go on to explore those other places. Here are a few options:

▶ You can work into just the front or just the back loop of the next stitch.

▶ You may skip stitches, work between stitches, around posts (see below), in spaces, in rows below, or into the side of existing stitches.

▶ You may work into previous stitches on the same row or into stitches on previous rows.

▶ You can even take your hook out of your work and insert it into a different spot altogether!

. . . .

Q Where do I put my hook when it says "back loop only" or "front loop only"?

A The *back loop* of a stitch is the one that is further away as you look at the work. The *front loop* is the one closer to you. Inserting into one or the other gives a completely different look to the stitch.

sc in front loop

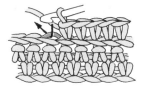

sc in back loop

Q What is a *post*?

A The post is the vertical part of the stitch, on stitches tall enough to have a vertical part. (Single crochet stitches aren't tall enough to have a post.)

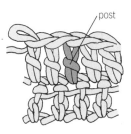

post

double crochet post

Q What is *front post double crochet* and *back post double crochet?*

A These stitches are created by putting your hook around the post of the next stitch on the previous row instead of into the top loop. Often crocheting around the post is alternated with single crochet.

For front post double crochet. Yarn over hook; keeping hook in front of work, insert hook from right to left around post of next stitch and pull yarn through loop; *yo, pull through two loops on hook; repeat from * once.

front post double crochet

For back post double crochet. Yarn over hook; keeping hook in back of work, insert hook from right to left around post of next stitch and pull through loop; *yo, pull through two loops on hook; repeat from * once.

back post double crochet

. . . .

Q Do I need to adjust my turning chain for front post and back post double crochet?

A Because working around the post brings the new stitch down into the previous row, it creates a shorter-than-normal height for the row. You may need to chain only one or two stitches to reach the needed height for your next row. If you are alternating front/back post double crochet with single crochet stitches, just chain one.

Q **How do I put my hook between stitches?**

A Instead of inserting the hook under the top V of the stitch, insert it in between the posts of the stitches on the previous row. This creates a more open fabric (and a different gauge) than stitching into the tops of the stitches.

inserting hook between posts

Q **How do I work into a space?**

A Usually the space you are working into was formed by one or more chain stitches, such as when you're working a granny square. Insert the hook under the entire chain stitch and pull up a loop from around the other side of the chain.

working into a space

Q What is the *row below?*

A The row below is the next-to-last row you completed. The *previous row* is the last row you completed — in other words, the row into which you are currently working.

··

Q What is a *spike stitch?*

A A spike stitch is a stitch that is worked into the row below or two rows below, rather than into the top of a stitch from the previous row. It "spikes" down into the fabric, partially covering a previous stitch. To work a spike stitch, you need to recognize

working into a stitch in the row below

the spot where the next stitch in the previous row was worked. You may be working into that same spot or into the stitch two rows below that stitch, depending on your pattern.

··

Q How do I count stitches?

A Take a close look at your work and learn to recognize how each stitch is made:

▶ **For the row you just worked.**
The top of each stitch looks like a sideways V, so if you count the Vs, you are counting stitches. Do not count the loop on the hook as a stitch.

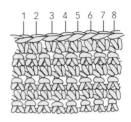

counting stitches in current row

▶ **For previous rows.**
Count each bump of a single crochet or each post of a double or treble crochet, plus the turning chain (if your pattern directed that it be counted as a stitch).

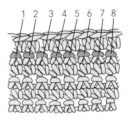

counting stitches in previous rows

▶ **For highly textured yarn.** You may have to count stitches as you work them or use your fingers to feel and count the bumps. (Each bump is a stitch.)

 How do I count rows?

As you get familiar with the look of the various stitches, this will get easier for you.

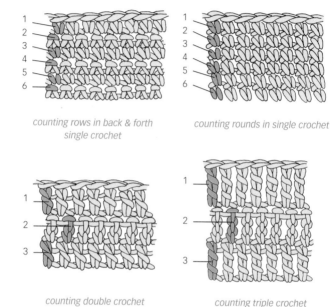

counting rows in back & forth single crochet

counting rounds in single crochet

counting double crochet

counting triple crochet

▶ **For back-and-forth single crochet.** Look for the distinct line between each pair of rows.

▶ **For in-the-round single crochet.** Look for the distinct line between each round.

▶ **For double and triple crochet.** Count each row or round of posts.

Q **How do I work into a slip stitch?**

A First, be sure that you are indeed supposed to work into it. Most commonly, slip stitches are used to move the yarn inconspicuously to a different spot in the work without intending to work into the stitch at a later time. Other times, slip stitch is meant to join rounds. In either case, you are not meant to work into the slip stitch. If you are certain that you are supposed to work into the stitch, take care to work loosely enough when making the slip stitch so that you are able to insert the hook into the stitch on the next row or round.

Q **My stitches are so tight I have trouble getting the hook into them on the next row. Can you help?**

A It shouldn't be difficult to put the hook into the stitches. If you are struggling to maneuver your hook, consider the following:

▶ Is the size of your hook appropriate for the yarn or thread you are using?

▶ Are you keeping too much tension on the yarn? Some crocheters use a tight tension in an effort to make their stitches even. Not a good idea!

▶ Is there tension on the yarn between the ball and your hand? Pull out some extra yarn so that the only tension comes between your yarn hand and the hook.

Concentrate on allowing the yarn to flow through your fingers.

▶ Are you making the stitch on the throat of the hook instead of on the shank? You may find it easier to use a hook with an inline head and a straight shank.

Decreasing and Increasing

Q How do I *decrease* a stitch?

A The best way is to work the stitch until just before there are two loops on the hook (the last step). Work the next stitch in the same manner. Yarn over and pull through all loops on hook. Study the illustrations below for what that means for the single, half double, and double crochet:

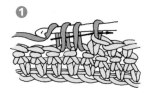 

▶ **Single crochet decrease (sc dec).**

1. (Insert hook in next stitch, pull up loop) twice.
2. Yo and pull through 3 loops on hook.

▶ **Half double crochet decrease (hdc dec).**

1. (Yo, insert hook in next stitch and pull up loop) twice.

2. Yo and pull through 5 loops on hook.

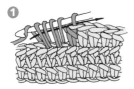
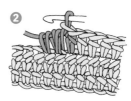

▶ **Double crochet decrease (dc dec).**

1. (Yo, insert hook in next stitch, pull up loop, yo and pull through 2 loops on hook) twice.

2. Yo and pull through 3 loops on hook.

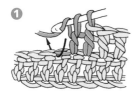
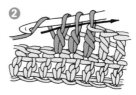

Q How do I make a decrease when I have to make a turning chain at the beginning of a row?

A Work the turning chain first, and then work the decrease over the next two stitches in the row.

Q How do I *increase* stitches within a row?

A Just work more than one stitch into the same stitch, giving them a common base. You can do this at the edge of a row or anywhere in the middle of a row or round.

increasing in single crochet

You may also work one or more chains between stitches as an increase. The increase creates a hole, so it is most commonly used as a part of a larger stitch pattern. Work these chains as stitches on the next row or round.

....

Q What if I need to increase a large number of stitches at the beginning of a row?

A Chain the required number of stitches at the end of the previous row to act as a foundation chain, plus enough to act as a turning chain.

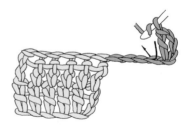

increasing several stitches at beginning of row

Work the first stitch into the chain as you would on a foundation chain, then work into each chain as a stitch and continue on across the stitches from the previous row.

How do I increase a large number of stitches at the end of a row?

When you finish working the row, insert the hook into the lower left-most loop (right-most loop for Lefties) of the stitch just made, and create a stitch. Continue working into the side of each stitch just made until you reach the desired number of stitches.

increasing several stitches at end of row

(This is the same procedure that you use for working foundationless stitches.)

SEE ALSO: *Pages 66–68, for foundationless stitches.*

Specialty Stitches

Q **What is an *extended (Elmore) stitch*?**

A Extended stitches, sometimes called Elmore stitches, are taller, slightly looser versions of the standard stitches. Each of the customary stitches can be extended to create a stitch with an intermediate height. These transitional stitches may be used to create smooth curves or to create a looser fabric than is possible with the standard stitch patterns. Extended single crochet is also known as *double single crochet*. Create an extended stitch by adding an extra "yarn over, pull through loop" step to a basic stitch pattern, as follows.

EXTENDED SINGLE CROCHET (ESC)

1. Insert hook into stitch. Yarn over and pull up a loop. Yarn over and pull through 1 loop on hook.

2. Yarn over and pull through 2 loops on hook.

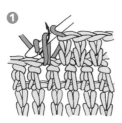
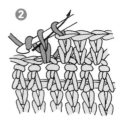

EXTENDED DOUBLE CROCHET (EDC)

1. Yarn over. Insert hook into stitch.

2. Yarn over and pull up a loop. Yarn over and pull through 1 loop on hook.

3. Yarn over and pull through 2 loops on hook.

4. Repeat last step.

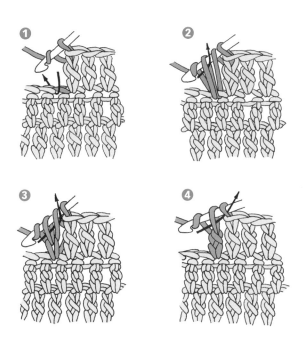

Q What is a *shell stitch?*

A A shell, or *fan,* stitch is a group of stitches worked into the same base stitch. Crowding the base of the stitches into one spot forces the top of the stitches to spread out into a shell or fan shape. They are usually worked with an uneven number of stitches so that there is a center stitch. Each

shell stitch

stitch of a shell counts as an individual stitch. There are many varieties of shell stitch patterns.

. . . .

Q What should I do if my shell stitch looks crowded and I can't really see the scalloped effects?

A If you are working from a published pattern, be sure you are reading the instructions carefully. Because the top of the stitches need room to spread, it is necessary to leave space on either side of the shell. Be sure to skip enough stitches between shells to show off the pattern.

. . . .

Q Why is there a hole at the base of my shell?

A The many stitches going into the same base stitch cause the base stitch to become stretched, creating a little hole. If you don't like the hole, try to stretch that stitch as little as possible while making your shell stitches. If you are making up your own shell stitch design, try making shells with fewer stitches.

Q What's the difference between a popcorn, bobble, and puff stitch?

A Each of these related texture stitch patterns is made by working multiple increases within a small space, then decreasing within that same space. The result is a stitch pattern that pops out of the surrounding fabric. They are usually made using a variation of double crochet; the number of stitches determines the size of the popcorn, bobble, or puff. Although they are made up of multiple stitches, when completed, each is counted as a single stitch. The difference among these stitch patterns is how the increases and decreases are made, and how the stitch pattern looks when complete.

Designers may use different names for the same technique, and each technique has its own variations. Be sure to check your published pattern for specific instructions for the techniques used in that pattern.

How do I make a *popcorn* stitch?

 You can work popcorn in double, half double, and treble crochet. Here's how:

1. Work several stitches into the same base stitch. When all the stitches have been worked, take the hook out of the loop. Insert the hook from front to back through the top of the first stitch of the popcorn.

2. Put the loop back onto the hook, yarn over and pull through the 2 loops on the hook to force the popcorn to "pop" off the background stitches.

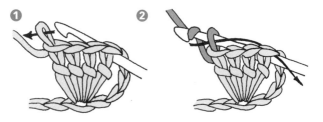

Q **Can I make my popcorn stitch appear on either side of the fabric?**

A Yes! When you take the hook out of the stitch, reinsert it into the stitch from front to back, and the popcorn goes to the front of the work. If you insert it from back to front, the popcorn ends up on the back of the work.

Q My popcorn stitch seems too loose and floppy. Can I make it look neater?

A Here are some ways to neaten your popcorn stitch.

▶ Work the stitches on a slightly smaller hook than you have been using for the rest of the stitching.
▶ Make your popcorn stitch over fewer stitches.
▶ Make a bobble instead of a popcorn.

Q How do I make a *bobble?*

A Work several stitches into the same base stitch, but omit the last step of each stitch. After you have worked the desired number of stitches, yarn over and pull through all the loops on the hook.

For example: Yo, insert hook into next stitch and pull through loop, *yo and pull through 2 loops on hook, yo, insert hook into same stitch and pull through loop; repeat from * two more times, yo and pull through 2 loops on hook, yo and pull through all 5 loops on hook.

Q Can I use popcorns and bobbles interchangeably?

A Although they don't look exactly the same, you can usually substitute a bobble for a popcorn and vice versa, since both stitches, when completed, count as a single stitch. However, be consistent: Don't substitute bobbles and popcorns willy-nilly throughout your fabric.

. . . .

Q How do I make a *puff?*

A A puff stitch is just a series of yarn overs and pulled-up loops worked into the same stitch.

1. (Yarn over, insert hook into stitch, and draw up a loop) several times, always into the same stitch. Yarn over and pull through all loops on hook.

2 & 3. Chain one to complete the puff and close the top of the stitch.

. . . .

Q **Why do my puff stitches look uneven?**

A It can take a bit of practice to control the size of the loops when making a puff stitch, but it's worth the practice! Work on a swatch until you are comfortable with the consistency of your stitches.

. . . .

Q **What is a *cluster*?**

A A cluster is made by working several partial stitches in a row, then finishing them all together with one final "yarn over, pull through all loops." The base of the cluster ranges over several stitches, but when the stitch is complete and all the loops are finished off together, it counts as a single stitch on the next row or round. The final effect of a cluster is to decrease a number of stitches.

For example: *Yo, insert hook into next stitch and pull up a loop, yo and pull through 2 loops on hook; repeat from * 2 more times, yo and pull through all 4 loops on hook.

. . . .

Q **Why is a cluster in one pattern different from other clusters in the same book?**

A The term *cluster* is used to denote many different stitch pattern variations. Always check your pattern for instructions particular to that pattern.

Q What is *crab* stitch?

A This stitch pattern is also known as *backwards single crochet, reverse single crochet, corded edging, lobster stitch,* and *shrimp stitch* (sounds like the menu at a seaside restaurant!). It is made by working a row of single crochet in the opposite direction from the usual method: In other words, from left to right for right-handers, and from right to left for Lefties. It is often used as an edge stitch, as it creates a beautiful border.

To work a row of crab stitch, first work a row of single crochet following the normal method, so that the edge lies flat. Do not turn at the end of the row. Chain 1, then single crochet in the last stitch of the previous row and in each stitch across. It may feel awkward at first, but after a few stitches you'll see a bumpy corded edge appear.

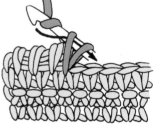

crab stitch

Q Is it possible to stitch into a row of backwards single crochet?

A No. Backward single crochet creates a corded edge that is meant to be the final row or round of a piece.

....

Q How do I crochet *cables?*

A Cables are made with a combination of stitches, often front post double crochet. At even intervals a stitch is worked several stitches forward or behind the current hook position. Your instructions indicate exactly how to make the cables.

....

Q What is a *selvage stitch?*

A A selvage stitch is a stitch at the beginning and/or end of a row that is not considered part of the stitch pattern. Not all stitch patterns contain selvage stitches, and many that do contain them do not identify them as such. They may be plain single or double crochet stitches that serve as a stabilizing "frame" for seaming or other finishing. Sometimes any stitch at the side edge of a piece is referred to as the selvage.

....

Q Can I begin a row without a turning chain?

A Yes! You might want to do this if you're starting a new color or to help in shaping.

1. Put a slip knot on the needle as if it were a loop from a chain.

2. Commence your stitch as usual.

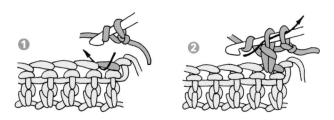

beginning a row without a chain

More About Stitches

Q What is a *stitch dictionary*?

A This is a budding designer's best friend! A stitch dictionary contains stitch patterns that you can mix and match to make your own creations. Each stitch pattern is clearly photographed and includes information on how many multiples to chain for the foundation row. Many stitch dictionaries contain both charted and text instructions.

SEE ALSO: *Page 193, for charts vs. text instruction.*

Q What is a *multiple?*

A A *multiple,* also called a stitch multiple, is the number of stitches required to work a complete stitch pattern widthwise. This set of stitches may be repeated across the width of the piece to create a pattern.

For example: A stitch pattern that uses a "multiple of 6 stitches" may be done over any multiple of 6 (including 6, 12, 18, and so on).

Some stitch patterns require a number of stitches in addition to the multiple in order to have (a) required selvedge stitch(es) or to center the stitch pattern on the fabric. If a stitch pattern calls for a "multiple of 6 plus 2," it means that the stitch pattern can be worked over any multiple of 6, plus 2 stitches (8, 14, 20, and so on).

Q What is a *pattern repeat?*

A A pattern repeat refers to the number of rows required to complete a stitch pattern lengthwise. A stitch pattern that is made by working the same eight rows over and over is said to have an eight-row pattern repeat.

Q What is the best way to learn a new stitch pattern or technique?

A Practice, practice, practice! Use a light-colored, smooth, worsted-weight yarn and an appropriate-sized hook — probably an H (5 mm). In the beginning, don't worry about your gauge or about making stitches look even. Work a little swatch until you are comfortable with the stitch pattern and your edges are even. Once you are confident with the stitch pattern or technique, you can start over to work a gauge swatch or to begin your project.

SEE ALSO: *Pages 123–25, for swatching.*

If you don't understand something the first time, try approaching it through one of your other senses. Everyone has a different style of learning that works best for that person. For instance, I'm a kinesthetic learner. Reading about techniques doesn't help me unless I have yarn and hook in hand so that I can *do* as I read. You may need to look at the pictures, because you are a visual learner. Or perhaps reading the instructions aloud helps because you learn best by hearing the words. It may help to have someone else read the instructions and explain them to you using *different* words. Whatever your learning style, do what it takes to understand a technique that is new to you.

Q The illustrations in the book look so clear, but when I look at my work, the stitches aren't as well-defined. How do I translate what I see in the book to my own work?

A It may be comforting to know that many others experience the same frustration. Realize that the illustrations must be simplified and idealized to be effective. If the illustrator drew a fuzzy strand of yarn, you wouldn't have a clue about where to put your hook! See if you can identify the main parts of the stitch, as drawn in the illustration; it doesn't matter if your yarn doesn't look exactly like the yarn pictured. You might find it helpful to have some smooth cotton yarn on hand to practice with.

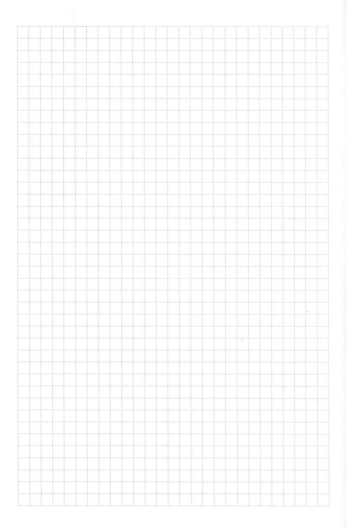

CHAPTER 5

Tense about Gauge?

IN THE UK, GAUGE IS KNOWN AS *tension,* a term that accurately reflects many crocheters' thoughts on the subject! Gauge is important, however, so let's take a moment to understand the concept of gauge and how to get it.

Getting Gauge

Q **Exactly what is *gauge?***

A Gauge is simply a description of how many stitches and rows a particular stitch pattern has within a certain area.

Q **What determines gauge?**

A Gauge is dependent on a number of factors, including hook size, yarn size, your individual way of handling hook and yarn, and even your mood at a particular moment!

Q **How is gauge stated?**

A Gauge may be expressed in stitches and rows per inch, or in stitches and rows per 4" (10 cm), with a suggested hook size. Sometimes the row gauge is omitted.

For example: 24 stitches and 28 rows = 4" (10 cm) in single crochet with J/10 (6.0 mm) hook

A gauge may also be stated in terms of complete multiples or motifs.

For example: Rounds 1–3 of granny square = 3" (7.6 cm) with H/8 (5.0 mm) hook

or

Two pattern repeats = 7" (17.7 cm) with H/8 (5.0 mm) hook

....

Q **Should I always use the hook size that is given in the pattern?**

A No, but it's a good starting point. It is the size the designer used to get the stated gauge, but every individual's handling of yarns and hooks varies. Even when using identical hooks and yarns, two crocheters can get very different gauges. If you need to change hook size to obtain a stated gauge, please do so. That does not mean that you are right and the gauge statement is wrong, but just illustrates the fact that gauge is achieved in a wide variety of ways.

....

Q **How do I figure out what my gauge is?**

A You'll need to make and measure a gauge swatch: a small piece of fabric made using the same yarn and hook you plan to use for your project.

Q How big should my gauge swatch be?

A Ideally, a swatch should be no less than 4" (10 cm) across; 6" (15.2 cm) or more is better. The thicker the yarn, the bigger the swatch you need. The finest thread crochet swatches can be somewhat smaller.

If you are working a stitch pattern with multiples, you'll need to make the swatch big enough to encompass at least one multiple.

SEE ALSO: *Page 117, for multiples.*

Q How do I make a gauge swatch?

A Start with enough chains to make an adequately sized swatch, taking care to work the chain loosely. Be sure to adjust the number of stitches to fit any stitch pattern multiples.

Begin stitching, using the stitch pattern given in the gauge statement and the same hook and yarn you plan to use for the project. Different hooks, even those of the same size, handle yarn differently. Even different colors of the same yarn may work up to different gauges! Because the same yarn in different colors can yield different gauges, use all the colors in the same way you plan to use them in the finished product, if you are using more than one color.

Work in the same way the project requires (in the round or back and forth), unless otherwise stated in the pattern. Crochet at least 2" (5 cm), then measure to see if you are anywhere close to the desired gauge. If not, stop stitching. End off and begin with a different size hook on a new swatch. If you are close, continue stitching until your piece is about 6" (15.2 cm) long.

. . . .

Q **How do I measure stitch gauge?**

A Place the swatch flat on a table. (Voice of Experience: *Do* use a flat surface, not your leg or the sofa cushion, as these surfaces aren't really flat.) Place a ruler on top of the swatch. (A ruler is preferable to a tape measure because it lies flat and doesn't stretch.) Measuring from the 1" (2.5 cm) mark, count the number of stitches to the 5" (12.5 cm) mark (that is 4" [10 cm] worth of stitches). Don't count the outer stitch or two on either edge and don't measure the first two rows or the last row, as

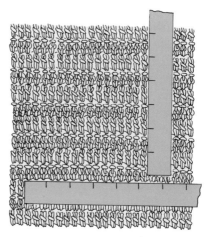

measuring a swatch

these edge stitches are often uneven or distorted. If you don't have 4" (10 cm) worth of stitches, use what you have. The more stitches you can count over a longer distance, the more accurate your results will be. Divide the number of stitches by the number of inches for your gauge per inch.

· ·

Q How do I measure row gauge?

A The technique is the same as for stitch gauge, but place the ruler vertically rather than horizontally on the swatch.

· ·

Q What should I do if my gauge doesn't match the gauge given in the instructions?

A If you did not get the gauge you wanted or expected, do not fiddle with the swatch to make it conform to your wishes, no matter how tempting! Instead, repeat the process, substituting hook sizes as necessary, until you are confident that you have determined the correct hook size to give you the gauge you need.

· ·

Q What if I have too many stitches and rows per inch?

A Switch to a larger hook to loosen up the work, which will give you fewer stitches per inch.

· ·

Q **What if I have too few stitches and rows per inch?**

A Switch to a smaller hook to make the stitches tighter, which will result in more stitches per inch.

....

Q **What if I have the right number of stitches per inch, but not the right number of rows per inch?**

A It may not matter much, if you are close. If the pattern calls for you to work to a certain number of inches before shaping, you may be able to adjust the length of your piece without worrying about row counts.

Row gauge does matter in some cases. If you are working a stitch pattern with a large row repeat as well as a stitch multiple, the placement of the rows becomes more important. For example, if the stitch pattern tells you to start shaping at Row X, row gauge matters.

If you really need to match the row gauge, try going up or down hook sizes. Sometimes this will change the row count but will not perceptibly change the stitch count. If that doesn't work, try switching brands or types of hook, using the same size that you used to get the correct stitch gauge. If the stitch pattern allows, you might be able to adjust the row gauge by working a row of extended stitches (edc vs. dc, for example) every row or every other row.

You may also be able to adjust your row gauge by making the loop you pull up through the stitch slightly longer or shorter than you normally would. However, you will have to pay attention and remember to do this consistently throughout the entire piece in order to maintain a constant row gauge.

SEE ALSO: *Pages 106–7, for extended stitches.*

Gauge Matters

Q **What should I do with my swatch after it's finished?**

A Stop and write down what hook you used. Be specific: for example, "aluminum Susan Bates H/8 (5 mm)." Also note the name and color of the yarn, how many stitches and rows your swatch has, and what the stitch pattern is (or where it can be found in a book).

If you're close to having your desired gauge, block your swatch as you will your finished project, then measure again to make sure the gauge hasn't changed.

SEE ALSO: *Pages 237–45, for blocking.*

Q **Why should I block my swatch?**

A Sometimes washing and blocking changes the gauge. Unless you plan never to launder your finished item, you'll need to know how these processes affect the fabric.

If it's a multicolored item, you also need to know if the colors will run. And you need to know all this before you spend hours on stitching.

· ·

Q **Why should I take measurements before and after blocking my swatch?**

A The "after blocking" gauge is the one that matters the most, because that is what the finished gauge will be. Imagine how you would feel if you stitched a whole sweater and found out the gauge changed after you washed it!

Be sure to note the gauge before blocking, and label it before washing it. This is the gauge that you'll have while you are stitching the fabric. Next, block your swatch and make note of the finished gauge. It is this finished gauge that needs to match the gauge stated in your pattern, unless the pattern instructions say otherwise.

· ·

Q **Do I rip out my swatch now that I have gotten the right gauge?**

A I wouldn't — at least not immediately. If you are running short of yarn at the end of your project, you may need to rip it out, but in the meantime, keep it around for reference. You may need to recheck your gauge down the road. Some yarns aren't readily ripped out and reused, so attempting to unravel the swatch would be pointless. When you've collected enough swatches, you may decide to make a patchwork afghan, bag, or other item.

. . . .

Q How should I measure a thick-and-thin yarn? Aren't the results likely to differ from place to place?

A If you are using a thick-and-thin yarn, or have a complex stitch pattern, measure again elsewhere on the same swatch and compare the results. If the gauges are different, take an average.

. . . .

Q Why do published patterns always remind me to "take time to check gauge"?

A It does save time to get the correct gauge. How long does it take to do a really good gauge swatch? And how long does it take to make a sweater, put it together, try it on, find it doesn't fit, rip it out, and re-stitch it? Case closed.

. . . .

Q You're kidding. I have to do all this preparation every time?

A It's not that bad! The effort you put forth on the swatch end of things is in direct proportion to the time, money, and effort you put into the finished product. Getting the correct gauge is crucial to the success of many crochet projects, but not all. Only you can determine how much work you are willing to do in the early stages.

If you are making a scrap yarn afghan out of bits and pieces and don't care how big it is, just dive right in without swatching. Similarly, if you are making a potholder or doily, don't worry about it. On the other hand, if you are making a sweater that needs to fit a real body, it is very important to get the right gauge. In that case, time spent on the swatch is time well spent. Let's look at an example of a sweater.

Gauge in instructions: 4 sc per 1" (2.5 cm)
Desired finished bust measurement: 42"

You therefore need 4 sts × 42" = 168 stitches for the circumference of the sweater. If you are even just a half stitch off per inch (2.5 cm), it can make a huge difference. Here are some examples:

▶ If your gauge is 3½ sc per inch (2.5 cm) and you follow the pattern instructions as written, your finished sweater will be 168 sts ÷ 3½ = 48" around, or 6" (15 cm) too large!

▶ If you work the same sweater with a gauge of 4½ sc per inch, the finished sweater will be 168 sts ÷ 4½ = 37" around, or 5" (12.5 cm) too small!

Q If I don't care about exact measurements, are getting gauge and blocking my stitch necessary?

A Maybe. For instance, if you are working with several different colors, washing a swatch can alert you to the possibility that colors may bleed. Also, if your gauge is off you may find yourself short of yarn. Stitching at a different gauge uses up yarn at a different rate.

....

Q Help! I made a bunch of swatches but didn't label them. How can I tell them apart?

A It's probably too late for this, but in the future put a paper hang tag on each swatch as you work it. Note all the information pertinent to that swatch on the tag, and you'll thank yourself for your organizational skills!

....

Q What if I can't obtain the gauge that is called for in the pattern instructions?

A Sometimes, no matter what you do, you just can't match the pattern's gauge. If you've tried everything — from changing hook sizes and/or brands to checking to make sure you are following the instructions correctly — you may have to go with your gauge and make adjustments accordingly.

....

For example: The pattern gauge is 16 sc = 4" (10 cm), with 80 stitches in the first row to make a fabric 20" (50 cm) wide.

Your gauge is 15 sc = 4" (10 cm), or 3.75 sc = 1" (2.5 cm).

$$15 \text{ sc} \div 16 \text{ sc} = .9375$$
(your gauge) ÷ (pattern gauge) = (conversion factor)

$$80 \text{ sts} \times .9375 = 75 \text{ sts}$$
(pattern number) × (conversion factor) = (revised number)

Check the math:
75 sts ÷ 3.75 sc per inch = 20" (50 cm) wide

. . . .

Q **How do I adjust for a different gauge?**

A If your gauge is just a little bit off from the pattern's gauge (or if you like the fabric you get with your gauge more than with the given gauge), you can adjust the stitch numbers throughout the pattern. First, figure the conversion factor by dividing your new gauge by the gauge given in the pattern. Every time the pattern gives you a number of stitches, multiply the number by the conversion factor.

. . . .

Q Why do the instructions give two gauges?

A Different stitch patterns result in different gauges. If a project has more than one stitch pattern, the directions specify gauge for each and you need gauge swatches for each.

. . . .

Q Do I have to match the gauge on the yarn band?

A No. The gauge information given on the yarn band is just a starting point to give you an idea of what weight/size/category yarn you have and what an appropriate hook size might be for that yarn. You might find you are happy with fabric you make using that gauge, or you may find you want to adjust it to suit your preferences. If you are following a published pattern, it's more important to match the gauge given in the instructions than the gauge on the yarn band.

. . . .

Q The gauge on my project isn't the same as on my swatch. Why is this, and should I worry?

A Ask yourself these questions:

▶ Did you do a large enough swatch to become accustomed to the yarn and the stitch pattern? Sometimes gauge changes as we become more familiar with a stitch pattern.

▶ Are you sure you measured your swatch accurately? Did you "cheat" to get the right gauge? Did you measure over at least 4" (10 cm)?

▶ Did you work your gauge swatch in the same stitch pattern you are working now? With the same hook? With the same yarn, in the same color?

▶ Have you consulted your notes? If you blocked your swatch, the gauge may have changed after blocking. If your "before" gauge is the same as what you are currently working on, you can be confident that you are on target.

▶ Could the weight of the work be elongating the stitches as the piece gets heavier? Try supporting the work on your lap as you stitch.

▶ Are you under any more, or less, stress than when you made your swatch? The stitches you made while relaxing at your mountain cabin may be different from the stitches that you make at the end of a hectic workday.

. . . .

Q **Is it a problem that my gauge changes throughout my swatch?**

A Yes. Try to keep an even tension on the yarn while you are working. Be sure you are holding the yarn the same way throughout. Keep working until your swatch looks even; it may take a while to become accustomed to the stitch pattern and yarn. Once you are satisfied with the uniformity of your stitching, continue working until the swatch is large enough to measure over the evenly stitched portion of the fabric.

. . . .

Q I put down my afghan for a year, and when I came back to it, my gauge had changed. What happened?

A Life. You may be more relaxed or more tense than you were when you last worked on it. You may have become more confident in your technique. You may not have used the same hook. Just change to whatever hook size you need to match your new stitches to your previous work.

CHAPTER 6

Going in Circles . . . and Squares and Triangles

CROCHETING BACK AND FORTH IN ROWS is not the only way to go! Many crocheted pieces are worked in rounds rather than rows. This method produces both flat motifs, such as granny squares, and seamless three-dimensional items, such as hats.

Good Beginnings

Q How do I start a flat piece in the round?

A The technique for working a flat piece in the round is the same whether you want your finished piece to be a circle, square, triangle, or other shape:

1. Start with a crocheted chain, and then join the chain with a slip stitch to form a tiny circle (called a *ring*).

2. Work a beginning-of-the-round chain to raise the hook to the correct height for the first round, depending on what height stitch you plan to work. Work the first round into the ring.

Q How many stitches should be in my starting chain?

A It's usually 4 or 5 stitches, just enough to get the required number of stitches into the ring on the first round, but no more. That number is surprisingly fewer than you might think. In general, a joined chain-4 ring easily holds 8 stitches. A chain-5 or -6 ring holds a dozen or more stitches.

....

Q Can I make a large hole in the center of the piece?

A Just start with a longer chain and put more stitches into the ring on the first round. Feel free to experiment with different numbers of chains in your starting ring.

....

Q What does it mean to work *into the ring?*

A Instead of putting your hook into a chain stitch, as you do for back-and-forth crochet, put your hook into the center of the ring and pull up a loop around the chain. As you work the stitches, hold the yarn tail near the chain and work around it as well to secure the tail.

SEE ALSO: *Pages 151–52, for starting a flat piece.*

Q How many stitches go into the first round?

A That depends on both what you want your final shape to be and the height of your stitches. The taller the stitch, the more stitches you need to put into the first round. Here's why: The larger a circle's diameter, the longer its circumference. The circumference of the circle is measured at the top of the stitches. Because taller stitches create a wider circle as compared to smaller stitches, more stitches are required to make a longer circumference. You'll note that the taller stitches may be crowded together at their bases, but spread out at their tops to form a circle.

SEE ALSO: *Page 143, for formulas.*

Q What happens at the end of the first round?

A You have two choices: either *closing the round* or *working in a spiral.* When you close the round, you join the last stitch in the round to the first stitch with a slip stitch.

You may also keep working in a continuous spiral without closing the round. Be sure to place a marker in

closing the round

the last stitch of the round and move it out on each subsequent round so that you know where the beginning of the round is. You still have to work increases on each round of the spiral in order to keep the piece flat.

working in a spiral

Q **How do I keep my motif flat?**

A Each subsequent round requires a number of increases in order to keep the piece flat, because as a circle gets larger, more stitches are needed to fill the widening circumference.

Q **How do I determine how many stitches to increase each round?**

A The height of the stitches determines the number of the stitches you need to increase on each round. The taller the stitches you are working, the more increases you need to make.

SEE ALSO: *Page 143, for formulas.*

Q Where do I put the increases?

A The placement of the increases determines the shape of the motif. When you space the increases evenly, you create a circle. If you group the increases at four equidistant positions, you create a square. You can make other shapes by placing increases at other points.

SEE ALSO: *Pages 142–43, for circles; pages 143–44, for squares; page 144, for other shapes.*

Q What kind of increase should I make?

A Any kind you want. You may work multiple stitches into the same base stitch, make one or more chain stitches, or use a combination of stitches and chains.

Working Various Shapes

Q How do I make a flat circle?

A If you start with the correct number of stitches in the first round, it is fairly simple to keep up with the required increases. Increase in every stitch on Round 2, every other stitch on Round 3, every third stitch on Round 4, and so on.

Basic Formula for a Circle

	SINGLE CROCHET	HALF DOUBLE CROCHET	DOUBLE CROCHET	TRIPLE CROCHET
CHAINS	4	4	4	5
STITCHES IN RING FOR ROUND 1*	6	7	11	17
INCREASES NEEDED FOR EACH ROUND	6	8	12	18
STITCHES AT END OF ROUND 2	12	16	24	36
STITCHES AT END OF ROUND 3	18	24	36	54
STITCHES AT END OF ROUND 4	24	32	48	72

*Not including beginning round of chain.

Note: *In half double, double, and triple crochet, the beginning-of-the-round chain is counted as a stitch; in single crochet it is not.*

. . . .

Q **How do I make a flat square?**

A Begin with a chain ring as for a circle, but instead of spreading out the increases evenly, group all the increases at just four locations evenly spaced around the ring.

Basic Formula for a Square

	SINGLE CROCHET	HALF DOUBLE CROCHET	DOUBLE CROCHET	TRIPLE CROCHET
STITCHES IN RING FOR ROUND 1	6	7	11	15
INCREASES NEEDED FOR EACH ROUND	6	8	12	16

*Not including beginning of round chain.

Note that a single crochet square offers special challenges, since you need to space six increases evenly at four locations. You can play with the math until it works out for your design: Put 12 increases evenly spaced every other round or increase 6 every round, alternating the corners where you put double increases.

. . . .

Q **How do I make other flat shapes?**

A You can make triangles, hexagons, and other flat shapes following the same system as for a square. Begin with a chain ring and group all the increases together: in 3 spots for a triangle, 6 for a hexagon, and so on. You may need to change the number of stitches in your starting ring or your first round in order to make the stitch counts work out evenly.

. . . .

SINGLE CROCHET TRIANGLE

Work through Round 1 of a single crochet flat circle.

RND 2: Ch 1, *3 sc in next sc, sc in next sc; repeat from * one more time, 3 sc in next sc, join.

RND 3: Ch 1, sc in next sc, * 3 sc in next sc, sc in next 3 sc; repeat from * one more time, 3 sc in next sc, sc in next sc, join.

RND 4: Ch 1, sc in next 2 sc, * 3 sc in next sc, sc in next 5 sc; repeat from * one more time, 3 sc in next sc, sc in next 2 sc, join.

RND 5: Ch 1, sc in next 3 sc, *3 sc in next sc, sc in next 7 sc; repeat from * one more time, 3 sc in next sc, sc in next 3 sc, join.

DOUBLE CROCHET TRIANGLE

Ch 4, join with slip stitch to form ring.

RND 1: Ch 3 (counts as dc), 11 dc in ring, join. [12 dc]

RND 2: Ch 3, dc in next 2 dc, *5 dc in next dc, dc in next 3 dc; repeat from * one more time, 5 dc in next dc, join. [24 dc]

RND 3: Ch 3, dc in next 4 dc, *5 dc in next dc, dc in next 7 dc; repeat from * one more time, 5 dc in next dc, dc in next 2 dc, join.

variation on double crochet triangle

RND 4: Ch 3, dc in next 6 dc, *5 dc in next dc, dc in next 11 dc; repeat from * one more time, 5 dc in next dc, dc in next 4 dc, join.

Q How do I make an oval?

A An oval or oblong shape uses elements of both back-and-forth and circular stitching. Essentially, you are making two semicircles at either end of a straight piece of crochet; the increases are grouped at the ends. The number of increases you need depends on the stitch pattern that you are working. For example, single crochet requires 6 increases every round to remain flat, so $6 \div 2 = 3$ increases at each end.

CROCHETING A SINGLE CROCHET OVAL

1. Work a foundation chain. Turn. Work two single crochet into the second chain from the hook. Single crochet across to the last chain.

2. Work 3 single crochet into the last chain. These increases spread out around the end of the chain.

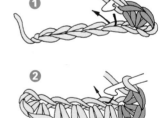

3. Rotate the piece so that the bottom half of the foundation chain turns to the top. Keeping the right side of the work facing you, work one stitch into each stitch on the opposite side of the foundation chain, including the chain where you put the first 2 single crochet. If you like,

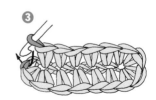

you may now choose to join the round with a slip stitch. Place a marker in the last stitch. (Remember to move this marker each time you complete a round.)

4. Work Round 2, increasing in each of the next 2 stitches, then work straight until you get to the 3 stitches at the other end. Work 2 single crochet in each of those 3 single crochet, then work straight to the last stitch of the round and work 2 single crochet in that stitch. (You have increased 3 stitches at each end.)

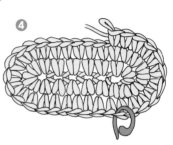

From here on out, you get to eyeball it. Keep an increase at the very end of each curve, and make the other two increases evenly spaced at increasingly wider distances from the center of the curve. It's not rocket science: As long as the oval lies flat, you're doing it right.

. . . .

 I'd like to work an oval in double crochet. How many increases do I need?

 A double crochet oval requires 12 increases every round (6 increases at each end).

Problem-Solving Flat Shapes

Q **I followed the chart, but my piece isn't flat. What did I do wrong?**

A This is a common problem. Here are some things you can check:

If your crochet is curling into a bowl shape:

▶ You may not have started with enough stitches, or you may not have made enough increases per round.

▶ Even though you are increasing sufficiently, you may be working the stitches too tightly. Loosen up a bit or try a larger hook. It is even okay to change hook sizes when stitches change within the same motif, if that's what it takes to make it lie flat.

If the motif is ruffling:

▶ You may have too many increases per round.

▶ If after counting your stitches, you find your numbers are right, you may be working the stitches too loosely. Try a smaller hook.

▶ Consider making each stitch slightly taller. For example, try an extended double crochet in place of a double crochet.

SEE ALSO: *Pages 106–7, for extended crochet.*

While the charts give general guidelines for working a flat motif, you may find you need to bend the rules a bit based on your crocheting style and personal preferences. Be assured that it is okay to add or subtract increases as you work, in order to have the piece lie perfectly flat. This is especially true on the bigger rounds when working larger pieces.

Q Can I use more than one kind of stitch when I'm working a flat motif?

A You can certainly mix stitch heights on your motifs. Just remember to change the number of increases accordingly. For example, you start a circle using double crochet stitches, increasing 8 stitches each round. If on one round, you want to use treble crochet, you must increase 18 times in that round in order to maintain a flat circle.

Q Is there another way to keep my pieces flat when I'm working in the round?

A If you prefer to be more relaxed about your stitching, you can be. Keeping in mind the guidelines above, experiment with doubling the increases every other round, or in some other arrangement. Remember that you can use a combination of chains and stitches for your increases, and that you can use a chain-space in place of a stitch, as for a granny square. Just be sure to stop at the end of every round, place your piece flat on a table, look at the outside edge, and check to see that it remains flat. Be honest with yourself!

Turning a blind eye won't help: If your piece is not flat on Round 3, it won't correct itself on Round 6.

If you notice that the last round you worked is not quite right, sometimes it is possible to make adjustments on the following round without ripping out the problem round. If you aren't happy with the adjustment round, stop! Rip out both rounds and get it right before continuing. (Voice of Experience: From someone who abhors ripping out stitches — sometimes it just has to be done.)

. . . .

Q **Where do I put my hook when working in rounds?**

A When you work back and forth, turning the work at the end of each row, you put your hook into loops lying sideways just slightly *to the left* of the next stitch. On the other hand, when working in rounds without turn-

placement of hook when working in the round

ing, you put your hook into loops lying sideways just slightly *to the right* of the next stitch.

> *Note: If you turn your work to the other side, you'll see this is the same spot you've been putting it in when working back and forth. The difference is that you are always seeing the right side of the fabric when you work in rounds.*

. . . .

How do I squeeze in all the stitches I need in the first round?

A Be sure you are not letting the bases of the stitches overlap one another. When they overlap, you can't slide them around the ring easily. If they aren't overlapping, yet there still is not room for them all, add one more chain to your beginning round or try one of the alternate beginnings described below.

. . . .

Q Can I make a smaller center ring?

A To get a closed center, try these alternate ways of beginning a circle:

WORKING ROUND 1 INTO A YARN RING

1. Leaving about a 6" (15 cm) tail, wrap yarn into a ring around your finger as if to start a slip knot. Insert hook into ring.
2. Yarn over hook. Pull up a loop. Proceed to work the first round of stitches into the ring as you would into a crocheted ring.

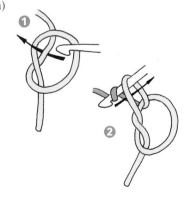

(cont'd on next page)

151

3. When you have the desired number of stitches on your first round, tug the non-working tail of the yarn to tighten the hole.

WORKING ROUND 1 INTO AN EXTRA CHAIN

1. Chain 2, 3, or 4 (for single crochet, half double crochet, and double crochet, respectively). In effect, this is a turning chain plus one stitch.

2. Work Round 1 into the first chain you made. (You are working all the first round stitches into the extra chain.)

3. Pull tail to close center.

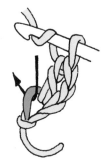

working into extra chain

Q **How can I improve the knot at the beginning of a circle?**

A Try beginning with one of the knotless methods above, or instead of using the end attached to the ball when working the initial slip stitch, try using the tail end of the yarn.

Q What can I do to improve the slip stitch join at the end of a round?

A If you think the join is sloppy, try this alternate method of joining: Work to the end of the round, but before joining with a slip stitch, remove the hook from the loop. Insert the hook into the spot you want to join as if to make a stitch, pull up the loop you just dropped, and continue. If you still don't

pulling loop through back to front

like the way it looks, try it again, inserting the hook into the stitch from back to front and pulling through the loop.

· ·

Q Why does my circle look like a spiral instead of separate rounds?

A When you work the rounds, you are probably failing to join the last stitch of round to top of chain at beginning of round. Although you sometimes may want to crochet a spiral, if not, be sure that you start each round with a beginning chain in order to raise hook to correct height. This beginning chain counts as a stitch. When you've reached the end of the round and made the appropriate increases, join round with a slip stitch to top of beginning chain.

SEE ALSO: *Page 140, for stitch heights of beginning chains.*

Q Do I have to use both a joining stitch and a beginning chain when working rounds?

spiral

A In crochet, you don't have to do anything! Some circularly made items, both flat and cylindrical, are worked in continuous flat spirals. Be sure to place a marker to help you identify the end of the round.

Q How do I find the end of the round?

A If you are joining rounds, put a stitch marker in the top loop of the chain that begins the round. If you are working without joining rounds, slip the marker onto the first stitch of the first round. The next time around, when you work a stitch into the marked stitch, move the marker into

placing a marker on a joined round

placing a marker on a spiral round

the new stitch, and continue to move the marker on each subsequent round.

....

Q **Why isn't my circle exactly round?**

A You may be stacking the increases on top of each other on each round. Try moving the increases so that they occur at different places on each round.

═══

Granny Squares

Q **What's the difference between any old square and a granny square?**

A The familiar granny square is a special form of square motif. Although there are many variations on the granny square, the traditional one is a double-crocheted square made with a series of chains and double-crocheted blocks — a kind of filet crochet in the round.

Granny squares can be worked with any number of colors. They are a great way to use up scraps. They can be made with any size yarn and hook, and can be made with any number of rounds. Make a single granny square big enough and you have an afghan!

....

Q How do I make a granny square?

A You could just follow the general instructions above for a double-crocheted square, but since granny squares are so popular, I'll make it easy for you and give you a pattern.

TRADITIONAL GRANNY SQUARE

With MC, ch 4, join with a slip stitch to form ring.

RND 1: Ch 3 (counts as dc), 2 dc in ring, *ch 1, 3 dc in ring; repeat from * two more times, ch 1, join to top of ch-3. Cut MC and end off.

RND 2: Attach CC in any chain space. (Ch 3, 2 dc, ch 1, 3 dc, ch 1) in chain space, *(3 dc, ch 1, 3 dc, ch 1) in next space; repeat from * two more times, join to top of ch-3. Cut CC and end off.

RND 3: Attach MC to any space between groups. (Ch 3, 2 dc, ch 1) in chain space, *(3 dc, ch 1, 3 dc) in next space, ch 1; 3 dc in next space, ch 1, repeat from * two more times, (3 dc, ch 1, 3 dc) in next space, ch 1, join with slip stitch. Break MC.

See how you are increasing 3 stitches in

each of the four corners, with groups of 3 dc in each chain space? With each additional round, you continue to work increases in the corners separated by groups of 3 dc in between. You can continue doing that *ad infinitum*.

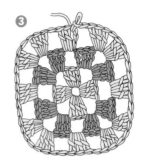

. . . .

Q I like the way granny squares look, but I don't like all those yarn ends. What's a good way to manage the ends when working multicolored motifs?

A Work them in as you stitch. When you start a new round in a new color, leave about 6" (15.2 cm) of the old color. Hold the tail of the old color at the base of the next stitch. As you insert your hook to make the next stitch, work around the tail of the old color. Do this for several stitches until you think the tail is secure, then drop the old color tail. You can go back and trim the ends later.

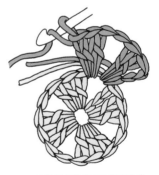

working tails in as you stitch

Q Are there other kinds of squares?

A There are hundreds of variations of square motifs, as well as circles and hexagons. Entire books have been written on the subject. Once you are familiar with the concept of making flat motifs, you'll want to design your own.

. . . .

Q How can I get more pronounced points at the corners of my motif?

A Try placing a taller stitch in each corner stitch of the motif. In other words, if you are making a double crochet square, place a treble crochet in place of the center double crochet in each of the four corners. If the corner is made with a chain, make one extra chain. Experiment, as you may not need to make this adjustment on every round to get the look you want.

Working Other Shapes

Q I tried making a semicircle by working back and forth and adding half the number of increases per round needed for a circle, but the straight edge wasn't straight. Why?

A The tops of the stitches have room to spread out when you work this way, whereas in a full circle, they are crowded together and thus forced to stay in place. To solve the problem, make sure your increases are not at the edges of the semicircle, and use fewer than half the increases you would use for a circle in that stitch. For a double crocheted semicircle, crochet as follows:

CROCHETING A SEMICIRCLE

ROW 1: Beginning with one of the closed-center starts described above, Ch 3 (counts as dc), dc 5 the first row, turn. [6 dc] (This is one-half the number of stitches required for Round 1 of a double crochet circle.)

ROW 2: Ch 3, 2 dc in next dc and in each dc across, turn. [11 dc] (This is one less increase than you make for a dc circle, resulting in fewer than half the stitches required for Round 2 of a dc circle.)

ROW 3: Ch 3, (1 dc in next dc, 2 dc in next dc) 5 times, turn. [16 dc]

ROW 4: Ch 3, (1 dc in next 2 dc, 2 dc in next dc) 5 times, turn. [21 dc]

Q I want to work a three-dimensional shape in the round. Is it possible to crochet a tube?

A Certainly! Crochet a foundation chain with as many stitches as you need for the circumference you desire. Making sure the chain is not twisted, insert the hook into the first stitch of the chain

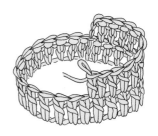

crocheting a tube

and work a slip stitch to form a ring. Work a beginning chain to raise the hook to the appropriate height, then work into each stitch around. At the end of the round, join with a slip stitch to the top of the turning chain. Repeat this round for as many times as required to get the desired length.

. . . .

Q My tube isn't straight. What makes it skew?

A This is a common problem, inherent in the stitching. It happens because the stitches are not exactly on top of each other. Because you are working in the same direction all the time, there is no opposite pull on the stitches to straighten them out. You can prevent the skewing by turning your work after joining at the end of each round.

. . . .

Q How can I make my motifs crisp and neat?

A There are a couple of refinements you can make in order to make tidier motifs:

▶ Instead of starting each round in the same place, end one round and start the next one in a different spot. This prevents the chains from stacking on top of one another, and works especially well when you are changing colors on each round.

▶ You can avoid stacked chains by starting new yarns without a chain, instead of using beginning-of-the-round chains.

SEE ALSO: *Pages 54–55, for joining a new yarn.*

CHAPTER 7

A Whole Cloth

IT'S TIME NOW TO EXPLORE THE FEATURES of crocheted fabrics and the techniques used to make them.

Search for the Perfect Fabric

Q Is *fabric* really the right word to use when talking about crochet?

A Like weaving or knitting, crocheting is a method of creating a fabric. It may be lightweight or heavy, lacy or dense, smooth or textured. It may drape fluidly over the hand, or stand stiffly at attention. These fabric characteristics are a function of stitch pattern, fiber, and gauge. While there is no one perfect crocheted fabric for every use, there are features that make various ones ideal for different purposes.

Q What is *drape*?

A The drape of a fabric is an expression of how the fabric hangs — how stiff or how supple it is. Several things influence the fabric's drape:

▶ **The gauge of the stitching in relation to the size of the yarn.** A tight gauge creates a stiff fabric.

▶ **The yarn itself.** Some yarn is naturally stiff, but it may feel less so after washing. Linen softens up considerably after washing, as do some wools. Wash and block your swatch and see how you like it then. Some less expensive synthetic yarns have a plastic-like feel that makes them more suited to craft projects than to crocheted or knitted garments.

SEE ALSO: *Pages 237–45, for blocking.*

▶ **The stitch pattern.** Single crochet fabric is stiffer than double crochet fabric. If you are having trouble getting a fabric you like with the basic stitches, try working an extended stitch to see if that loosens things up, but be aware that it may change your gauge.

SEE ALSO: *Page 76, for extended stitches.*

▶ **Your technique.** Relax! If your goal is a fabric with a nice, soft drape, be sure you are holding the hook gently and allowing the yarn to flow through your fingers. If the fabric is still too stiff despite your best efforts, switch to a different yarn.

· ·

Q **Is there a right side to my fabric?**

A Probably. If you are doing a highly textured stitch like cables or bobbles, the "interesting" side is the right side. When working in rounds, the smoother side is the right side. Ultimately, however, the right side is whichever side you want it to be.

Q How do I tell which is the right side when I'm working back and forth?

A Unless your pattern says otherwise, the first row worked after the foundation chain is usually the right side. You may want to hang a stitch marker on the front of the fabric, so you'll be able to recognize the right side from the wrong side on later rows.

Q Why are my edges uneven?

A You may not be keeping a consistent number of stitches on each row. Review the concept of using a turning chain as a stitch, and count your stitches after every row until you are confident that you are maintaining the same number.

SEE ALSO: *Page 88, for turning chains.*

Q I can achieve straight edges with most patterns, but I have difficulty when working ripple stitch. Is there anything I can do about this?

A You may not be working enough stitches into the beginning and ending of each row. Ripple stitch rows usually begin and end with several stitches worked into the same base stitch. Reread your pattern instructions to see if you are following them correctly.

 Q Why is my fabric getting wider?

A There are several things that may cause this:

▶ Your foundation chain may be too tight in relation to your stitch pattern. Rip out your work and start over with a looser foundation chain.

▶ You may be increasing unintentionally. If you are using a turning chain as a stitch, you may be putting your hook into the base of the chain in every row, which creates an increase.

▶ You may have relaxed your gauge as you became comfortable with the stitching. Measure the newest part of the fabric to determine if you need to change to a smaller hook.

▶ You may have picked up the wrong hook and started using a larger hook size or a different brand of hook. Have you borrowed the hook from this project to use in a different project? Check your notes to make sure you are using the same hook you started with.

Q **Why is my fabric getting narrower?**

A This is a common problem. Here are possible causes, with some easy solutions:

▶ You may be decreasing unintentionally. At the end of each row, make sure you are inserting your hook into the top of the turning chain of the previous row if the turning chain is counted as a stitch. Count your stitches after every row until you are confident that you are maintaining the correct number of stitches.

SEE ALSO: *Pages 87–90, for turning chains.*

▶ You may have tightened your gauge as you worked. Check to see if you need to change to a larger hook.
▶ You may have picked up the wrong hook and started using a smaller hook size or a different brand of hook. Check your notes to make sure you are using the same hook you started with.

. . . .

 Q **Why is there a hole where I've been stitching?**

A Here are several things to look for:

▶ You may have unintentionally skipped a stitch.
▶ If the hole is at the edge of the fabric, it could be caused by the turning chain. Try making the turning chain one chain shorter and see if that helps.

SEE ALSO: *Pages 87–90, for turning chains.*

▶ If the hole occurs where you've skipped a stitch in order to decrease, use a different type of decrease.

SEE ALSO: *Pages 102–3, for decreases.*

▶ If the hole occurs where you've worked many stitches into one, as in a shell stitch, that's just a part of the stitch pattern and is hard to avoid.

▶ If the hole occurs where you started a new yarn, fix the hole when you weave in the tail.

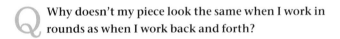

Q Why doesn't my piece look the same when I work in rounds as when I work back and forth?

A When you work back and forth, the two different sides of a stitch pattern show on alternating rows. When working in rounds, only one side of the stitch pattern shows.

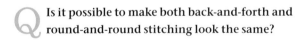

Q Is it possible to make both back-and-forth and round-and-round stitching look the same?

A Yes, it is. Here are some suggestions:

▶ **To make rounds look like back-and-forth fabric,** join the rounds at the end of each row, then turn, work a turning chain, and continue in the other direction. Doing this at the end of each round creates a fabric in which the front and the back of the stitch pattern show on alternating rounds.

▶ **To make back-and-forth fabric look like in-the-round fabric,** break the yarn at the end of every row and work from right to left only on each row (left to right for Lefties). This is more awkward than the first method, so plan ahead. If you are making a sweater in the round, it is easier to work the rounds below the armholes as described above. You can then work the sections above the armholes back and forth, maintaining the same visual appearance to the stitch pattern.

 Q Why is my rectangle skewed?

A A non-square fabric can stem from a number of sources:

▶ **Not using turning chains properly.** Be sure that all turning chains are the right height for the stitch you are using. If appropriate, treat the turning chains as stitches and work into them. If they are not treated as a stitch, do not work into them at the end of a row.

SEE ALSO: *Pages 87–90, for turning stitches.*

▶ **A stitch pattern that biases the fabric.** See if you can you work into the stitch pattern more loosely to alleviate the bias.

▶ **A yarn that biases the fabric.** A poorly spun, unbalanced yarn may cause problems. Try a different yarn to see if the swatch is still skewed. If your pattern allows, and it is the stitch pattern or yarn that is causing the bias, you might try working back and forth in the round to see if the opposite pull of the stitches straightens the fabric.

SEE ALSO: *Page 150, for working back and forth in the round.*

 How can I make a ribbed fabric?

Alternating stitches of front-post double crochet and back-post double crochet over several rows creates a ribbed fabric. Keep in mind that this type of ribbing does not have the same characteristic stretch as a knit ribbed fabric.

SEE ALSO: *Page 96, for front- and back-post double crochet.*

Working with Color

Q **How do I change colors within a row or round?**

A Follow this procedure on the last stitch before you want the new color to start:

1. Work until there are two loops on the hook. Leaving a tail of about 6" (15 cm) of the new color, yarn over hook with the new color.

2. Pull through both remaining loops on hook. Now continue on in the new color.

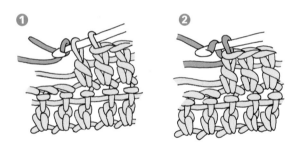

changing colors

....

Q **Why do my color changes look messy?**

A Make sure you are starting the new color soon enough; that is, when there are still two loops of the old color left on the hook. Do this even at the end of a row/round, when the first stitch of the next row/round will be in a new color.

If you have been securing the tail of the old color by working over it in the new color stitches, you may be getting some telltale color showing through. Wait until the piece is finished to worry about those ends, then work the tails into the back of the same-color stitches.

You could be having problems with the tension on the old and new stitches; if so, just adjust the size of the stitches when you weave in the ends.

....

Q How do I incorporate two or more colors on the same row or round?

A You work with only one color per stitch. The challenge is what to do with the other color. The solution depends on how far the other yarn has to travel to its next stitch. You may carry the unused yarn loosely across the back of the work (called *stranding*), catch it behind the stitches you are working, or drop it and start a new length of yarn for each section of color (called *intarsia*).

....

Q How do I strand colors?

A When you reach the color change, simply drop the color you just used (color A), pick up the new color (color B), and work a section in color B. When you pick up color A again, be sure to leave a bit of slack in the "float" behind color B so that the fabric is not distorted. You can carry both yarns across a row or throughout a round in this manner. If the floats are more than a few stitches wide, hold the unused yarn at the top of the previous row and work around this strand every few stitches when you are working with the other yarn.

If you have to carry the yarn a bit further, another option is to catch the unused color behind the base of every stitch you work, as you do when securing tails.

SEE ALSO: *Page 55, for securing tails.*

Q How do I work *intarsia?*

A Intarsia uses separate lengths of yarn for each section of color. Start by determining how many different color sections you will be working across the row, and cut a corresponding number of yarn lengths in the appropriate color. Each separate length of yarn should be about 2–3 yards (2–2.5 m) long. Work in the first color (Color A) as indicated, then drop Color A and begin the next color (Color B), allowing Color A to hang on the wrong side. When you have completed the B section, start with a new, separate length of Color A (or the next color), and continue across the row, using a separate piece of yarn for each color section. On the following row, the color of yarn you need should be waiting there for you to pick up as you come to each color change.

Q **How do I decide which method to use?**

A Sometimes this decision is a matter of personal preference. Stranding usually works well for two or three colors that alternate across a row. Hiding the unused yarn behind each of the contrasting color stitches allows you to switch back and forth easily between the two colors. However, because it creates a thicker fabric than intarsia, it is usually unsuitable for more than two colors at a time. It may also be difficult to hide a highly contrasting color within the stitches.

When you have large blocks of color, or units of color that are isolated, intarsia is usually the most appropriate method. Use intarsia when the length between colors makes it difficult to do stranding or when the number of colors used in a row would make stranding impractical.

As always, it's a good idea to practice your color technique on a swatch before beginning your project.

My yarn gets tangled on the wrong side when I work with colors. Am I doing something wrong?

You aren't doing anything wrong; it's just a feature of some types of color work. Some crocheters wind lengths of yarn onto yarn bobbins to make the yarns more manageable. Others prefer to cut long lengths of yarn and allow them to hang out and look messy on the wrong side of the work, pulling each strand free of its brothers as they work (my favorite). Still others prefer to use one of several types of commercially made yarn holders.

If you alternate the way you turn the work at the end of each row (clockwise one time, counterclockwise the next) the colors will untwist themselves every other row. This only works, however, if you don't twist the colors when you pick up a new color; just drop the old color and hold it to the right (Lefties: to the left) when you pick up the new color.

. . . .

Why does my fabric pucker when I'm working with different colors?

You are pulling the yarn floats too tightly across the back of the fabric. Take care to allow plenty of slack as the unused yarn travels across the back of the stitches. You may want to use one of the other color methods instead.

. . . .

Q **Can I carry unused yarns up the side of the fabric?**

A If the yarn doesn't have to travel very far (no more than a few rows), it's fine to carry an unused yarn up the side of a piece. Make sure you keep it loose, and catch it once or twice around a turning chain. However, cut the yarn and start it again if you are using lots of different colors. If carried vertically, several yarns together create too much seam bulk.

Q **How do I read a color graph?**

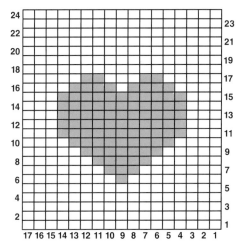

graph for pattern worked in rows

Each square in a color graph indicates one stitch as it appears from the right side of the fabric. Each row of the graph indicates a row or round of stitching. Starting at the lower right-hand corner of the graph (Lefties: lower left-hand corner), read each square from right to left (Lefties: left to right) for a right-side row. Turn the work, then read each square on the second row from left to right (Lefties: right to left).

If you are working in rounds, read every row from right to left (Lefties: left to right) since the right side of the fabric faces you at all times. If you are working back and forth in rounds to look like back-and-forth stitching, treat it as you do row-by-row stitching.

A graph often has lines indicating a pattern repeat. Work the area between the lines as many times as necessary, always working in the same direction.

Q **I'd like to try a pattern with a picture. Can you advise me on how to manage the colors?**

A Graphs indicate where to put the colors. When it's time to change colors, use the same method as for adding a new yarn: Work until the last two loops are remaining on the last stitch of the old color, then yarn over with the new color and continue working.

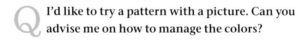

SEE ALSO: *Page 174, for stranding; pages 174–75, for intarsia.*

Better Shaping

Q Can I avoid stair-step shaping on the neck and armholes of a piece?

A Many published patterns give shaping instructions that leave a stair-step edge at the neck and armholes. It can be difficult to work with these jagged edges; a smooth curved edge is much easier to seam or finish with a border.

To refine the shaping of a curved edge, take advantage of what you know about stitch heights: decrease the height of the last stitch or two of a shaped

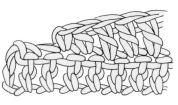

gradual shaping

edge. For example, on shoulder shaping your pattern might read: "Ch 3, dc to last 3 sts. End off." This creates a shorter row by omitting the last 3 stitches, but leaves an abrupt angle where the double crochet ends. Instead, you could work, "Ch 3, dc to last 5 sts, hdc in next st, sc in next st. End off." This creates a more gradual slope.

SEE ALSO: *Page 76, for stitch heights.*

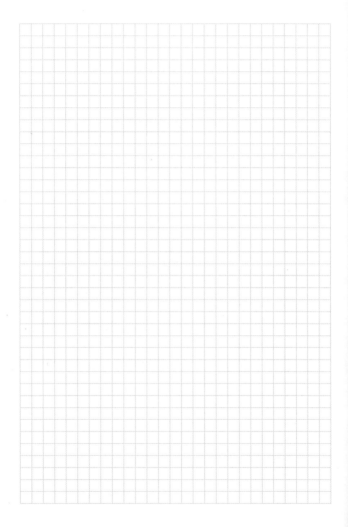

CHAPTER 8

Pattern Language

WHILE MANY CROCHETERS HAPPILY STITCH ALONG, making up their own projects without ever following a published pattern, others like to duplicate a crocheted item in a book or magazine. For this, you need to be able to follow written pattern instructions.

The Anatomy of Patterns

Q **Published patterns seem to be written in a different language! How do you go about "translating" them?**

A If you're put off by written instructions because they look complicated, think of them as a recipe. Most people are comfortable with reading recipes because they are familiar with cooking terminology and abbreviations. If you take the time to become comfortable with crochet jargon, you'll be well on your way to following any written pattern.

Q **What do well-written patterns have in common?**

A Although crochet patterns may not be standardized, well-written patterns have a lot in common:
  ▶ A materials list and gauge information, row-by-row (or round-by-round) instructions, and finishing instructions

▶ Often, a combination of text and symbols for stitch patterns, allowing you to choose the format that works best for you

▶ Information on yarn weight and content

▶ Gauge, usually over at least 4" (10 cm) in the main stitch pattern, and sometimes in all stitch patterns used in the project

▶ Suggested hook size to get gauge

▶ A range of sizes. The best patterns have complete information on sizes, including the finished chest measurement and length, sleeve lengths, neck width, and so on. Much of this information may be shown on a schematic drawing. The more information you have, the easier it is to make the garment fit well.

SEE ALSO: *Page 187, for schematic drawings.*

▶ Easy-to-read print, with text instructions that use standard abbreviations. Any special abbreviations or techniques are clearly explained.

▶ If applicable, information on stitch pattern multiples. This data simplifies pattern adjustments.

 I've never followed a pattern before — where do I begin?

 Start by looking at the preliminary section that describes materials needed, gauge, and size information. Take a

look at the schematic drawing, if one is given. Choose your desired size and a suitable yarn, then scan the how-to-stitch section for an idea of how the project is constructed. If it's a stitch pattern that's new to you, you may not be able to understand the row-by-row instructions until you have hook and yarn in hand.

. . . .

Q **What should I expect to see under "materials"?**

A This is the ingredients list of your crochet recipe — the items that you need to gather in order to make your project. It's a good idea to collect all of them before you begin stitching, although you may want to wait to purchase buttons until you can try them with your finished fabric. The materials list may include the following:

▶ Recommended yarn, including company name and name of yarn, yarn weight, size of balls/skeins, amounts in yards/meters, and fiber content

▶ Suggested size and type of hook(s). Remember: This is just a suggestion. Use the size you need to get the gauge called for in the pattern. If a hook other than a standard style hook is needed, the pattern will say so.

▶ Stitch markers, a tapestry needle, and any other tools you may need to complete the project. (Voice of Experience: Sometimes the pattern omits these items, especially scissors. You *always* need scissors.)

▶ Plastic rings, buttons, and any other trim items needed for the project

Q Why do I need to look at the gauge statement before I even get my yarn?

A If you have been crocheting for a while, you know that the suggested gauge can give you an idea of the size/weight of the yarn called for in the pattern. It also gives you an idea of how heavy the fabric will be and what kind of yarn you should use. In some cases, you may find (to your delight) that gauge is not crucial in the project.

Q Why are some sizes written within parentheses?

A When instructions for more than one size are given in the pattern, the numbers within the parentheses indicate the number of stitches or inches corresponding to a particular size. You may find it easier to follow the instructions if you circle your size with a pencil or highlight it with marker throughout. Here is a typical example:

Sizes: Small (Medium, Large, Extra Large)
Finished Chest Sizes: 38 (42, 46, 50)"

In the above example, the number for the smallest size is first, followed by the number for each subsequent size in that same order within the parentheses. In this example, size Small has a finished chest measurement of 38" (96.5 cm); size Large has a finished chest measurement of 46" (116.8 cm).

Sometimes both parentheses and brackets are used to denote several sets of measurements.

Sizes: Child's S (M, L, XL) [Adult's S (M, L, XL)]

. . . .

Q **Why are body measurements and finished measurements different?**

The difference between the wearer's body measurement and the finished sweater measurement is called *ease*. Ease is necessary for a good fit, but it varies according to the style of the sweater and the weight of the yarn. It may also take into account the wearer's preference for how the garment will fit.

Body-hugging sweaters have little ease, while more casual sweaters and coats have a great deal of ease. The outside measurement of a sweater made of bulky yarns may differ from its measurements inside, next to the body. Since measurements are taken on the outside of the garment, bulky sweaters must have more ease to result in the same fit as a sweater made with thinner yarn.

SEE ALSO: *Pages 188–89, for more on sizes and fit.*

. . . .

Q **What is a schematic drawing and why is it important to review it?**

A A schematic drawing is a graphic representation that includes the dimensions of the pieces of a project. It is often shown at the end of a pattern, but it is important to look at it before you start stitching because it contains a lot of useful information.

A schematic shows the shape and proportion of each stitched piece, so you can have an idea of what shape you are creating. It may show details like pocket placement and neck or edge treatments. If the garment is made in one piece, the schematic indicates that.

If the shaping of the front and back are similar, often only the front schematic is given. If the sweater is a cardigan, you may have only one-half of the front. Don't worry — there's still plenty of information given! You can look at a schematic and determine where you might need to make size adjustments: longer or shorter sleeves, wider neckline, and so on.

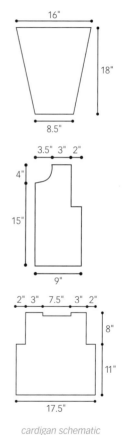

cardigan schematic

Size Matters

Q **How do I know which size to make?**

A Use all the information that the pattern instructions give you to determine what size is best for you. Look at the information about finished measurements that you find at the beginning of the instructions and in the schematic. Compare the finished measurements with a garment that fits you well and is of similar style and weight. Choose the size that results in the closest match to your desired finished chest/bust measurement. Remember, you can always shorten or lengthen the sleeves and bodies of garments.

If you don't have a finished garment to measure, look at the finished measurements and compare them to your actual body measurements. Take into account how much ease you will need to get the silhouette you want for that garment.

SEE ALSO: *Page 186, for more on ease and measurements.*

Q **What's the best way to take body measurements?**

A Measure over your normal undergarments. Measure over the fullest part of your chest/bust, making sure the tape measure is parallel to the floor. Hold the tape so that it is not slack, but don't pull too tightly either.

Also measure from the bone at the center back of your neck to your wrist ("Center Back to Cuff" measurement), and across

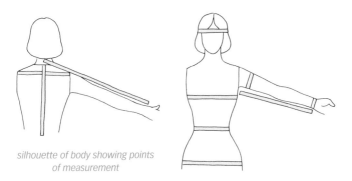

silhouette of body showing points of measurement

your shoulders from the tip of one shoulder to the tip of the other shoulder ("Cross-Back" measurement). Depending on the garment, you may want to know your upper arm measurement at the widest point, and/or your hip or wrist measurements. For length, measure from the bone at the center back of your neck to your waist or to your desired sweater length.

. . . .

Q **Can't I just assume that size Medium will fit me, just as it usually does?**

A Just because you wear a size 7 shoe, you wouldn't buy any size 7 shoe without trying it on! Don't assume you wear a size Medium because you always wear a size Medium. The medium size may just be the middle size given in the pattern. You need to determine what the designer means by "medium."

. . . .

Q **What if I need to make a sweater shorter or longer?**

A Unless you are working a complicated stitch pattern in which the row count matters, simply start any armhole shaping sooner (or later) than the pattern suggests. Start neck shaping when the height of the armhole is the same length as that given in the pattern. It is important to keep the distance between the beginning of the armhole shaping and the top of the sweater the same length as the original, because that measurement corresponds to the top-of-sleeve measurement. If you change the length of the armhole, you must also adjust the sleeve shaping. When adding length to a sweater, remember that you'll need more yarn than the pattern calls for.

Q **There are 10 rows in my stitch pattern. Do I need to change the pattern if I adjust the length of the body?**

A You have a couple of options. If the row count matters because of a stitch pattern, you'll have to take into account the number of rows it takes to finish a complete pattern repeat. Will the length be just about right if you simply add or subtract one pattern repeat? If not, you may need to start or end the stitch pattern on a different row.

Q What if I need to change the sleeve length?

A Changing sleeve length is a bit more complicated than changing body length, because sleeves are usually shaped from the cuff up to the shoulder. A change in sleeve length requires a change in the intervals between the shaping rows. A longer sleeve has more widely spaced increase rows; increase rows on a shorter sleeve are closer together.

Decide how long your sleeve needs to be. If it is less than an inch shorter than the given sleeve length, you may simply put a couple of the increase rows a bit closer together than the pattern suggests. If you need to make your sleeve just an inch longer, you may modify the pattern and crochet a couple more rows between two of the increase rows. However, if you need to change the sleeve length by more than about one inch, you need to do some math:

$$\text{Desired length of sleeve to widest point} - \text{Length of cuff or lower edge} = \text{Length available for shaping}$$

$$\text{Length available for shaping} \times \text{Row gauge} = \text{Number of rows available for shaping}$$

$$\text{Number of stitches needed to increase} \div 2 = \text{Number of times to increase on each side}$$

$$\text{Number of rows available for increase} \div \text{Number of times to increase on each side} = \text{How often to increase (in rows)}$$

"How often to increase" will probably not be a whole number. Just round it to the nearest whole number and increase that many times, or work increases on rows alternating between the two nearest whole numbers.

Pattern Talk

Q **What does "increase every sixth row" mean?**

A Work five rows even, then increase on the sixth row. Increases are on rows 6, 12, 24, and so on.

Q **Why are there special instructions?**

A Some pattern directions highlight information that is important for you to know before beginning. Be sure to read these carefully. Some examples you may run across include, "Yarn is used double throughout" and "Body of sweater is worked in one piece to underarm."

Q **Why is stitch pattern listed?**

A If a stitch pattern other than single, double, or treble crochet is used, it is often written out in full before the instructions for the piece. The stitch pattern multiple should also be given. The instructions usually tell you to work your gauge swatch in this stitch pattern.

SEE ALSO: *Pages 123–25, for gauge swatch.*

Q **Do I have to memorize all of those abbreviations and symbols?**

A Don't worry! Both text- and symbol-based instructions usually include a key explaining every abbreviation, symbol, or special stitch used in a project. Any unusual symbol is also accompanied by a text explanation of how to execute the stitch. If it's not listed on the pages right next to the project, look in the front or back of the book or magazine.

While there are some more-or-less standard abbreviations, standardization is relatively new to the crochet world. It's a good idea to check the abbreviations every time you start a new project. In time, you'll find you've memorized the most common abbreviations without even trying.

SEE ALSO: *Pages 282–86, for abbreviations.*

Q **Are subheadings important in a garment pattern?**

A Knowing where you are and what you are about to do is very helpful when making a sweater! Each portion of the garment is labeled: Front, Back, Sleeves. You may also see subheadings where shaping takes place, such as "Neck Shaping."

. . . .

 All these punctuation marks are giving me a headache. Why are there so many?

Your high-school English teacher was right: punctuation matters. In our written language punctuation marks show us where to pause and collect our thoughts before continuing on through a paragraph. In crochet patterns, they serve the same role by helping us move through a row. Each pattern publisher has its own punctuation style, but there are many similarities from pattern to pattern.

▶ **Periods** usually mean the end of a row.

▶ **Semicolons** are often used mid-row to set off a series of instructions.

▶ **Parentheses** may be used to denote sizes, as described earlier in this chapter.

▶ **Parentheses** are also used to set off stitches to be worked as a group. These sets are followed by a number indicating how many times to repeat the group. *For example:* (Yo, pull through 2 loops on hook) 3 times. means

Yarn over, pull through 2 loops on hook, yarn over, pull through 2 loops on hook, yarn over, pull through 2 loops on hook.

▶ **Parentheses** also may indicate steps to be done all into the same stitch.

For example: (sc, hdc, dc, hdc, sc) into ch-3 space.

means

Into the next space made by 3 chains, put a single crochet, half double crochet, double crochet, half double crochet, and single crochet, in that order.

▶ **Brackets or braces** may be used instead of, or in combination with, parentheses to set off more complicated instructions.

For example: [(dc in next dc, ch 1, skip 1 dc) twice, dc in next dc] twice

means

Into the previous row of double crochet stitches, double crochet, chain 1, skip 1 double crochet stitch, double crochet, chain 1, skip 1 double crochet stitch, double crochet (that's the first whole set written with brackets), double crochet, chain 1, skip 1 double crochet stitch, double crochet, chain 1, skip 1 double crochet stitch, double crochet.

▶ **Asterisks** indicate a point of repeat.

For example: Ch 1, sc in same stitch, * ch 1, skip 1 stitch, sc in next stitch; repeat from * two more times

means

Chain 1, single crochet in same stitch, chain 1, skip 1 stitch, single crochet in next stitch, chain 1, skip 1 stitch, single crochet in next stitch, chain 1, skip 1 stitch, single crochet in next stitch.

Some directions are worded "repeat from * twice," instead of "repeat from * two more times." Both examples mean the same thing: specifically, that you should work through the entire set of instructions from the asterisk (*) to "rep from" once, then repeat that section two more times, for a total of three times.

▶ **Repeat from * across row** means to work the instructions after the asterisk as many times as you need to in order to reach the end of the row. If you don't finish your row at exactly the end of the repeat, you've done something wrong.

However, **repeat from * to last 3 stitches, end sc in last 3 stitches** means that you are to repeat the pattern until there are only 3 stitches left in the row, then work one single crochet into each of the next 3 stitches to end the row. If you don't finish the repeated portion of the pattern with 3 stitches left to go on your row, you've done something wrong.

▶ **Daggers (†) and double asterisks (**)** are sometimes used in combination with other punctuation to designate repeated sets.

. . . .

 What if different punctuation marks are used in the same row?

This just means that there are multiple steps within a row. You still follow a prescribed order for the steps.

Start at the beginning of the row or round, and do each step as it comes. When you reach a set of parentheses or brackets, follow the sequences as described above as many times as necessary, then move on to the next step.

. . . .

Q **I thought I did what the instructions said, so why don't I come out with the right number of stitches at the end of the row?**

A Double-check your work to make sure you understood and followed the instructions correctly. Did you treat the turning chain properly, counting it as a stitch (or not), according to the instructions? Sometimes you can fudge a stitch or two to make it come out right, even if you did make a mistake. However, if you are going to be able to see the mistake, or if it will have undesirable consequences on future rows, you'll have to rip out the row and start again.

SEE ALSO: *Pages 87–90, for turning chain.*

Q **Why are there extra numbers at the end of a row? I don't have enough stitches to work them.**

A You may be confused by the stitch count at the end of a row. When the stitch count has changed during a row because of increases or decreases, most patterns give you an updated stitch count so you can check your number.

For example: You start with 21 stitches on a row. The next row says: Ch 3 (counts as dc), dc in same st, dc in next 19 sts, 2 dc in turning chain. [23 dc] You have increased one stitch at the beginning and at the end of the row, resulting in 23 double crochets.

Be aware that this stitch count number may be punctuated in a number of different ways. It may be in parentheses or brackets (as shown), or it may simply stand alone between periods or after a dash.

. . . .

Q I've tried and tried — why can't I get the pattern instructions to come out right?

A Of course, your pattern instructions may have a mistake! Here are some ways you can check yourself and the instructions.

▶ Try drawing each row/round out in symbols to see if it works.

▶ Try having someone read the pattern to you while you stitch, or try saying it aloud to yourself as you stitch.

▶ Ask for help from a more experienced crocheter.

▶ See if you can find an errata sheet for the pattern, either online or through the publisher.

▶ Above all, use your common sense. If you can see what the pattern is supposed to do, just go ahead and do it.

. . . .

Q I'm left-handed, and the instructions aren't working for me. What should I do?

A Most crochet instructions are written for right-handed crocheters — those who work from right to left across a row. Often it doesn't matter which way you work, but sometimes if you stitch from left to right across a row, the instructions don't work for you. Try substituting "left" for "right" and "right" for "left" in the instructions you are reading.

SEE ALSO: *Page 20, for more on left-handed crocheting.*

Q What does *RS facing* mean?

A RS is the right side of the fabric — the side you want to show to the public. When the instructions note the right side is facing you, it means that you are holding the piece with the right side toward you and you are about to stitch across it.

Q What does it mean to "end with a wrong-side (WS) row"?

A Ending with a wrong-side row means that the last row you work is a wrong-side row. Finish stitching a wrong-side row, then move on to the next step in the instructions, starting with a right-side row.

Q Why do some patterns have diagrams of stitches?

A In many countries, and increasingly in the United States, crochet instructions rely on symbols instead of, or in addition to, text to indicate placement of stitches. Each type of stitch is represented by a symbol that resembles that stitch.

. . . .

Q Why should I bother to read and become familiar with symbol crochet?

A Because the symbols resemble the stitches they represent, symbol crochet allows you to see what the stitch pattern is supposed to look like and to see the relationship of stitches to one another. Many crocheters find this way of presenting patterns easier to follow than written instructions. Having a visual aid can help you avoid mistakes before they happen.

Another advantage to learning this system is that you can read patterns from any country. For example, you'll find that stitchers in Japan are doing amazing things with crochet!

. . . .

Q How do I read a symbol crochet chart?

A Consult the chart key on pages 282–86 to become familiar with each symbol. Rows are numbered alternately on the left and right edges of the chart, indicating which direction each row is worked. Rounds are numbered along the right edge only. Begin with the required number of foundation chains (count them on the chart), and continue "reading the picture" as you make each stitch.

. . . .

Q How do I read a symbol chart if I'm left-handed?

A Symbol charts are written for those who stitch right-to-left. You'll have to remember to start each row on the opposite side of the chart.

. . . .

Q The instructions tell me to make a turning chain at the end of the row, but I'm used to making it at the beginning of a row. Which is correct?

A Either way is fine. Some patterns include the turning chain and "turn" instruction at the end of a row. Many newer patterns include these instructions at the beginning of the next row, as the turning chain often counts as the first stitch in the next row.

SEE ALSO: *Pages 87–90, for turning chains.*

Q How do I keep track of my place in patterns?

A Try one or more of the following techniques:

▶ Make a photocopy of your pattern and put a pencil mark on the copy as you finish each row (or each step). (Please make photocopies for your own use only — not for sharing with your friends.)

▶ Enlarge the pattern on a copier to make it easier to read.

▶ Use a magnet board and stand, moving the magnet up as you work each row.

▶ Use a sticky note to mark your place.

▶ Keep a notepad handy and jot down where you stopped.

▶ Buy a supply of hang tags and put them on your work each time you leave off, with a note reminding you where you left off. (Thanks, Maggie Righetti!)

▶ For complex stitch patterns or garment instructions, write each row on a separate index card. Punch a hole in the corner of each card and tie them together in order. Work Row 1 from the first card, flip it out of the way, work Row 2 from the next card, and so on.

▶ Practice "reading" your actual work so that you begin to see what needs to be done next. As you become comfortable with a stitch pattern, you'll develop the ability to work without referring to the written instructions.

How do I measure a curve when figuring armhole height?

You probably don't have to measure the curve. Even curved armholes and necklines are measured on a straight vertical line from the beginning of the shaping to the top.

. . . .

What's the difference between "dc in next 2 dc" and "2 dc in next dc"?

In the first example, you are putting a double crochet stitch into the top of each of the next two double crochet stitches. In the second instance, you are putting two double crochets into a single base — the top of a double crochet.

. . . .

What is the difference between "sc 1" and "1 sc"?

Probably nothing. Different pattern publishers have different writing styles.

Getting in Shape

Q **How do I accomplish "reverse shaping"?**

A Some shaping, such as for armholes or neck curves, takes place on one edge of the fabric. The instruction to "reverse shaping" means that you have worked one piece of a garment and now need to work a mirror image of that piece. You accomplish this by working the same directions for the second piece, but doing the shaping on the opposite edge of the fabric. For example, with RS facing, on a cardigan's Right Front, the armhole shaping is done on the left edge of the fabric and the neck shaping takes place on the right edge. The Left Front armhole shaping takes place on the right edge of the fabric and the neck shaping on the left.

To understand how the shaping works, you may find it helpful to draw out the shaping using symbol crochet, so you have a diagram of what's happening on both sides of the garment.

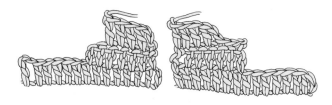

reverse shaping

SAMPLE SHAPING FOR A DOUBLE CROCHET CARDIGAN

For example, a typical pattern may read as follows:

Right Front: Work until piece measures 14" (35.5 cm) from beginning, ending WS row.

Armhole shaping:

(RS) Ch 3 (counts as dc), dc to last 7 dc, turn, leaving remaining stitches unworked.

(WS) Ch 1, slip stitch in same stitch and in next 2 dc, ch 3, dc in each stitch to end, turn. Work even until armhole measures 5½" (13.8 cm) from beginning of shaping.

Left Front: Work as for Right Front, reversing shaping.

Here's how to follow the above instructions:

On the Right Front, you work the first armhole shaping row by stopping short of working a full row. For the Left Front, work the same number of rows until you reach the armhole shaping. (Voice of Experience: Don't just measure. Count the rows.)

Now you are about to work a right-side row and need to shape the armhole at the beginning of the row, not at the end as you did for the Right Front. Here's how: Slip stitch across the first 7 stitches to move the hook and yarn across to the spot where you need to begin the row. (Remember: Slip stitches do not add height to a row.) You may also want to slip stitch into the next (eighth) stitch to put the yarn exactly under your chain. Now ch 3 to start the row, and work all the way to the end.

Next row (WS): Ch 3, work across the row until 2 stitches remain, turn, leaving remaining sts unworked. Work even until armhole measures 5½" (13.8 cm).

Q What does *continue in this manner* or *continue as established* mean?

A Say you've been increasing, decreasing, or working a particular stitch pattern. When you come to these instructions you simply keep doing what you've been doing, following whatever the immediately preceding instructions say to do.

Q How do I tell the Left Front from the Right Front of my sweater?

A Sweater pieces are described as they are worn, so the "Right Front" of a sweater is the piece for the front right side of your body. "Back Left Shoulder" is the part of the sweater Back that will be on your left shoulder when you wear the sweater. It's okay to hold pieces up to your body to figure this out!

Q What is difference between *Back* and *back*?

A Many patterns capitalize the parts of the sweater, so "Back" is a piece of a sweater. Lowercase *back,* on the other hand, usually refers to the work as you hold it: the "back" of the stitch is the side away from you or the "back" could be the wrong side of the fabric.

....

Q What does *end off* or *fasten off* mean?

A This is what you do to secure the last stitch and keep it from unraveling. Take your hook out of the stitch and cut the yarn, leaving at least a 6" (15 cm) tail. Pull this end through the last stitch and pull it tight.

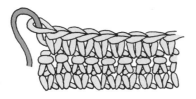

fastening off

Beyond Patterns

Q **How does copyright apply to me?**

A All written crochet patterns and articles are copyrighted, whether or not they say so explicitly. As such, they should never be photocopied without permission of the copyright holder. It is neither ethical nor legal to copy a pattern to give to your best friend, even if the pattern is no longer in print. It is neither ethical nor legal to make copies of instructions from a book so you can teach from it. And in many cases, it is neither ethical nor legal to buy a pattern and then crochet many copies of the item to sell at a craft fair.

If you want to obtain permission to photocopy a pattern, write to the publisher, who will put you in touch with the copyright holder. This may be the author or designer of the published pattern, or it may be the publisher.

There is one exception to the restrictions on copyrighted material: If you bought the pattern and would like to make a copy for yourself so that you can see it better or carry it conveniently in your crochet bag or make notes on it without altering the original, no special permission is required.

....

Q **How do I know if this pattern is too difficult for me?**

A Only you can determine that. Sometimes skill levels are suggested. If they aren't, scan the pattern to see if you recognize the stitches used. Ask yourself these questions:

- ▶ Is it well-written?
- ▶ Do I have the skills needed?
- ▶ If I don't have the skills needed, am I willing to learn them?
- ▶ Does it have shaping? If so, just a little or a lot?
- ▶ Is it an easy-to-see stitch pattern worked in an easy-to-see-yarn? Does that matter to me?

Don't let anybody tell you that you can't stitch something. If you are willing to learn new techniques, you can do it!

· ·

Q Where can I get free patterns?

A Yarn companies often give away patterns with a yarn purchase, and most have free patterns available on their Web sites. In fact, there are thousands of free patterns available on the Internet. Do a search for "crochet patterns," or look at Books, page 305, to get a start on finding free patterns.

Remember that patterns on the Internet may not have been edited for clarity and accuracy. If you are a beginning crocheter, you should probably start by using an edited pattern, either a purchased pattern for a publisher of books, magazines, or pamphlets, or one from a yarn company site.

CHAPTER 9

On the Edge

A CROCHETED BORDER CAN PROVIDE a stabilizing or decorative finished edge to a crocheted fabric. Many knitted sweaters have crocheted borders. There are even entire books dedicated to crocheted edgings.

Crocheting Borders

Q Where should I put my hook when picking up stitches along an edge?

A Always work the first row of an edging with the right side facing you.

▶ **If you are picking up along an upper horizontal edge** and the stitch gauge is the same for the border stitch pattern as for the main piece, you'll probably work into both loops on every stitch of the last row.

▶ **If you are working on the opposite edge of the foundation chain,** you are holding the piece upside down and stitching into the unworked loop of the foundation chain.

▶ **If you are picking up along a side edge,** you

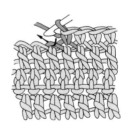

picking up along an upper horizontal edge

have to judge how far into
the edge and at what
intervals to put a stitch,
based on the fabric and
the size of the stitches you
are making. Insert the
hook into a stitch, rather
than into the space

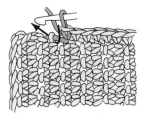

picking up along a side edge

between stitches. If you work into the space, you create
unsightly holes along the edge. If you are working a
single crochet border on the side of a single-crocheted
fabric, put a stitch in about every row of the edge. If you
are working a single crochet border along the side of a
double-crocheted fabric, you may need two stitches in
every row.

Q **What if the gauge of my border stitch pattern is not
the same as the gauge of my fabric?**

A You may have to make adjustments. On a horizontal
edge, using your swatch as a guide, experiment to see
if you need to stitch into 3 out of 4 stitches (for instance, one
stitch in next 3 stitches, skip one stitch), into 5 out of 4 (for
instance, one stitch into next 3 stitches, 2 stitches into next
stitch), or some other combination. Do the same thing along
a vertical edge, calculating how many stitches you need to put
into each row along the edge. Your goal is to crochet a border

that lies flat, without drawing in or flaring out. The most important thing is consistency. Take care to insert the hook the same distance into the fabric throughout the edge, and space the stitches evenly.

. . . .

Q **How do I "pick up stitches" evenly along an edge?**

A If you followed my earlier advice about making a swatch, you can use your swatch to help you. Using a ruler, place markers at 2" (5 cm) intervals along the edge of your swatch. If the border will be worked on both horizontal and vertical edges, be sure to mark both. Using the same number of stitches between each mark, stitch the border you'd like to use on your larger piece — if you are working from written instructions, there will be instructions for the border, possibly including the number of stitches to use. If you are adding a different border pattern, or if the specific instructions are not given, or if you cannot achieve the same gauge stated in the instructions, you may have to experiment to get the border to lie perfectly flat. When you are happy with the results, make a note of how many stitches you have within each 2" (5 cm) space on your swatch.

SEE ALSO: *Pages 123–25, for gauge swatch.*

Now mark 2" (5 cm) intervals on your larger piece and work the same number of stitches between the marks as you worked on your swatch. It's usually easy to keep track of the number of stitches within that short distance. (Voice of Experience: Of course, you may skip practicing on the swatch, but you'll have more to rip out if you don't get it right the first time.)

Q **Why doesn't my border lie flat?**

A It sometimes takes several tries to get this right. Start by analyzing what's happening, then you know what approach to take to correct it:

▶ If the border is ruffling, you may have too many stitches. Rip it out and start over with fewer stitches. You can also try a smaller hook.

▶ If the border is pulling in *(cupping)* you may need to rip it out, then use a larger hook and/or add more stitches.

Sometimes a border looks fine on the first few rows or rounds, but starts to misbehave as you work further. If this happens, use the same logic for adding or subtracting stitches described above to make it lie flat.

Q **Can I stitch a continuous border around a piece without turning?**

A Yes. Pick up and work stitches along each vertical and horizontal edge as described above, but when you reach a corner or a curve, you have to make certain adjustments. (See the next question.)

Q How do I make my corners lie flat?

A Think about turning a corner in a car: The outside wheels have to travel farther than the inside wheels to make the turn. The same principle applies when you work an edging on a crocheted piece. The outside rows/rounds have to travel farther than the inside rows/rounds, so you have to add stitches to increase the distance along the outer edge at each corner.

For example, on the first row/round of a single crochet border, work 3 single crochet into each corner stitch. When you finish these 3 stitches, mark the center stitch of the sc3 group, then when you come to that center stitch the next time around, work 3 single crochet stitches into it.

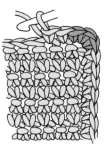

increasing in the corners

If you are working double crochet, put 5 stitches into the corner stitch. On the final row/round of a border, you can put fewer increases at each corner to soften the edge.

Q Why won't my neck edge lie flat?

A Make sure you are happy with the look of the first round/row of edging you worked. Does it lie flat?

Are there the same number of stitches on each side of the neck? Are both sides of the front neck symmetrical? If so, on the next rounds/rows, you may need to do the opposite of what you do on outside corners. A neckline is a circle that gets smaller as the width of the neck border increases. Each subsequent round/row of the border needs to be a bit smaller than the previous ones. Putting a few decreases on each round/row usually solves the problem. The best place to put these decreases is usually in the front and back "corners" of the neck and at either shoulder.

Q **I tried to pick up stitches evenly along my edge, but the first row still looks sloppy. How can I fix it?**

A It can be difficult to make the first row or round of an edging look good, especially if it is in a contrasting color. You are making decisions about where to put each stitch, and if you have to skip a base stitch here and there, the result can be an uneven-looking edge. Work the first row/round with the same color as the main portion, then stitch subsequent rows/rounds with the contrasting color. Be sure you have measured and are picking up stitches evenly and consistently throughout.

SEE ALSO: *Page 166, for horizontal and vertical pick-up on edges.*

Q How do I make a *picot edge*?

A A picot edge is a nice touch for a child's or woman's sweater, and it's very easy to make. Begin by working a row/round or two of single crochet along the edge. If working in rounds, join with a slip stitch. Work the picots on the final row/round as follows: *Sc in next sc, ch 3, sl st in same st, sc in next 2 sc; rep from * to end of row/round. Join with a slip stitch if working in rounds, and fasten off.

Q How do I make a *shell edge*?

A This classic edge is a great choice for any crocheted piece. Begin with a base row in a multiple of 6 stitches plus one. If you are working in the round, begin with a multiple of 6.

▶ **To work the final row:** Chain 1, skip first stitch, *skip 2 stitches, 5 dc into next stitch, skip 2 stitches, slip stitch into next stitch; repeat from * across. End off.

▶ **To work the final round:** Work as described above, but end the last repeat of the pattern by working a slip stitch into the top of the ch-1.

Q What if I don't have the right multiple of stitches for shell stitch on my pick up row/round?

A You can work an additional row/round of single crochet, increasing or decreasing a few times as needed to give you the desired multiple. Or, just adjust the edging a bit, adding or subtracting a stitch between the shells to make it come out right. As long as it looks good to you, it's right.

About Buttonholes

Q **Where do I put buttonholes?**

A Current fashion dictates that buttonholes go on the right front for women and on the left front for men. (I always have to go to the closet to check my other garments when it's Buttonhole Time.)

Even if you are following a pattern that gives instructions for buttonhole spacing, it's a good idea to double-check before working the buttonholes. This is especially true if you have added or subtracted length from the sweater, as you'll also have to adjust the buttonhole spacing.

Top and bottom buttonholes are usually ½" (1.25 cm) to 1" (2.5 cm) from the beginning of neck shaping and from the lower edge. If you are adding a neck border after the button border, take into consideration the width of the neck border; you may need to place the top buttonhole in the neck border and space the others evenly between. Most published patterns include this information.

Of course, buttons don't have to march in an evenly spaced, tidy line down the front of your sweater. You can use a single button at the neck, or put groups of 2 or 3 down the front. Use your imagination!

....

Q How do I space buttonholes evenly?

A Start by determining the placement of your top and bottom buttonholes. Mark these places with a stitch marker, coil-less safety pin, or piece of thread. You now have a couple of options for figuring the spacing for the remaining buttonholes:

OPTION #1: THE MATH-WHIZ WAY

1. With the crocheted piece flat on a table, measure the distance between the markers at the top and bottom of the garment.

2. Divide this distance by the number of remaining buttonholes, plus one. That is, if you need four more buttonholes, divide by 5.

3. Using a ruler, place markers at the intervals you determined in Step 2.

OPTION #2: NO MATH REQUIRED

This method works if you have an odd number of buttonholes. I always try to have an odd number of buttonholes so I can use this method!

1. Fold piece in half so that the top and bottom buttonhole markers are together.

2. Place third marker at fold; unfold the garment.

3. Fold again so that center marker and top marker are together.

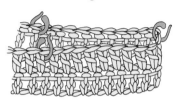

4. Place fourth marker at fold and unfold.

marking buttonholes by folding

5. Fold again so that center marker and bottom marker are together.

6. Place fifth marker at fold, and unfold. If necessary, continue to split the difference between the markers until the desired number of holes is marked.

Q **How do I make a *chain-and-skip buttonhole*?**

A This is a most popular buttonhole. It works well for single and half double crochet bands, but may be too loose for double crochet or taller stitches. It's easy to adjust the size of the buttonhole for different size buttons: just skip additional stitches and work additional chains. Start with a base row of single crochet.

CHAIN-AND-SKIP BUTTONHOLE

1. Place markers at each spot where you want a buttonhole.

2. Single crochet to the marker, chain 1 (or more), skip 1 stitch (or more — skip the same number of stitches as you made in your chain), single crochet to next marker.

3. Repeat steps 1 and 2 until all buttonholes are complete, then work to end of row/round.

4. On the next row/round, put one single crochet into the chain space for each stitch skipped.

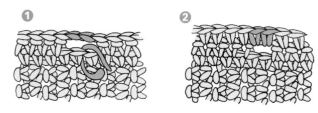

Q **Are there other buttonhole techniques?**

A A *simple chain loop* is easy to execute and can be sized to fit any button. It is worked on the final row of a band, but it may stretch out or be too flimsy for some fabrics. To make a chain loop buttonhole, follow Step 1 under chain-and-skip buttonhole above, then work to the buttonhole mark, chain the minimum number of stitches required to reach around the button, stretching it slightly, then stitch in same stitch or in the next stitch, and continue working band to next mark.

A *covered chain loop* is stronger and looks more finished than a simple chain loop. Here's how to do it:

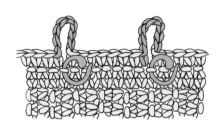

chain loop buttonhole

1. Make the covered chain loop on the last row of the border by working past the buttonhole marker, then chaining the number of stitches needed to go around the button. Remove the hook from the chain and insert it into the border several stitches back, then into the last chain made, so that the loop is centered over the marker.

2. Single crochet into this chain loop as many times as necessary to cover it, then continue with the border until the next buttonhole marker. Practice this on a swatch and try it with your button before working it on your finished garment.

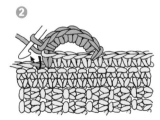

Q How do I know which buttonhole method to use?

A Remember that swatch? When you are checking the button band stitch on the edge of the swatch, go ahead and practice some buttonholes at the same time. You can try making different-sized buttonholes on it until you get one that looks pleasing, is stable, and exactly fits your button. If possible, it's best to buy your buttons before making the buttonholes. Then you can choose the method that works best for your garment/button combination.

Who's Got the Button?

Q Do you have any advice about choosing buttons?

A Choose a button in keeping with the style of the garment. Bulky outerwear usually requires large buttons, while lightweight lacy cardigans call for dainty buttons. If you are designing your own garment or want to make changes to a published pattern, before beginning the garment, decide whether you want the buttons and button bands to be a part of the design of the sweater or to be unobtrusive. Calculate the number of buttons you need by deciding how much space you want between buttons. Modesty may require more buttonholes on a garment meant to be worn next to the skin, which has little ease built into the design, while outerwear, which normally has more ease and is worn over other clothing, may require fewer buttons. If your sweaters often gap across the bust, an extra button or careful placement of buttons can prevent that dreaded "gaposis."

SEE ALSO: *Page 186 for ease.*

 I have rather large buttons and I'm having trouble aligning the buttonholes with them. Any tips?

 Keep in mind that the marker marks the center of the buttonhole. Larger buttons may require a chain-and-skip buttonhole that starts a stitch or two before the marker. If you make the buttonholes first, taking care to space them evenly, you can sew the buttons on to match the buttonholes.

How big should my buttonhole be?

A buttonhole should be only as big as it needs to be in order to get over the button. Buttonholes that are too big look sloppy and don't hold. Loop-style buttonholes often stretch, so they may need to be a bit smaller in the beginning.

Q **Is it possible to crochet buttons?**

A There are several ways to make a crocheted button. Here are three:

CROCHETED RING BUTTON

1. Leaving a 6" (15 cm) tail, single crochet around a purchased "bone" ring as many times as you can. If you have a big ring, you may need to make an additional round or two of single crochet.

2. Cut the yarn, leaving an 8" (20 cm) tail. With a tapestry needle, thread the longer tail through every single crochet around.

3. Pull the threaded yarn tight, bringing stitches to inside of ring. If necessary, take a couple of stitches across to tighten center. Use both ends to sew onto button band.

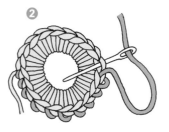

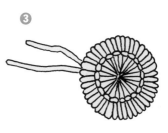

CROCHETED STUFFED BUTTON

Leaving an 8" (20 cm) tail, ch 2, join with slip stitch to first chain.

1. Round 1: Ch 1, 8 sc in ring, join.

2. Round 2: Ch 1, sc into slip stitch, *sc in next stitch, 2 sc in next stitch; repeat from * around, join with slip stitch. [12 sc]

3. Round 3: Sc in each sc, join.

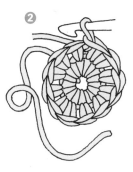

4. Round 4: Ch 1, *pull up a loop in next 2 sc, yo and pull through all loops on hook (dec made); repeat from * around, stuffing ball with a length of the same yarn before finishing round. End off and cut yarn, leaving a 10" (25 cm) tail.

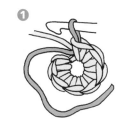

Thread tail through all stitches on last row and pull tight. Thread the 8" (20 cm) tail down through center of button and use both ends to sew button to fabric.

TINY BALL BUTTON

1. Round 1: Leaving an 8" (20 cm) tail, ch 2. Sc 7 in second ch from hook. *Do not join.*

2. Round 2: 2 sc in each stitch around. End off. Pull beginning tail to tighten hole and bring tail to inside. Thread ending tail around back loop of single crochet stitches.

3. Round 3: Roll tail into a ball for stuffing. Pull threaded tail tight, tacking together as necessary to form ball.

4. Round 4: Use ending tail to sew to fabric.

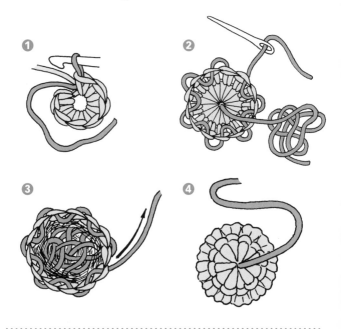

Can I fix a button band that seems too heavy for my sweater?

Try using a larger hook and correspondingly fewer stitches. If you aren't happy with the results using a single crochet band, you might try a *Granite Stitch Band:*

ROW 1: Single crochet evenly across, ending with an odd number of stitches.

ROW 2: Ch 1, sc in same stitch, *ch 1, skip next stitch, sc 1; repeat from * across row, turn.

ROW 3: Ch 1, sc in same stitch, *sc into ch-space, ch 1, skip 1 sc; repeat from *, end sc in ch-1 space, sc in sc.

Repeat Rows 2 and 3 as many times as desired, adding chain-and-skip or loop buttonholes as needed.

. . . .

What's the best way to sew on a button?

Sew it on just the way you would any button, using sewing thread in a color to match your yarn or your button. You can also use colored embroidery floss. Thread the sewing needle and knot the ends of the thread together so that the thread is doubled. Insert the needle from the back of the fabric to the front, up through the button and back down, then back into the fabric. At this point, if you put the needle through the loop made by the beginning knot, you'll prevent the knot from slipping up through the fabric. Make sure the threads are smooth and snug against the button, then continue sewing. When you have made several passes through the button, take a couple of small stitches on the back of the button band and cut the thread.

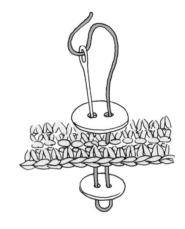

reinforcing button

If your fabric is flimsy or your button will get hard use, you may want to reinforce the stitching by adding a backing, such as another button or a piece of fabric or felt on the wrong side of the fabric. Stitch through the reinforcing button on the wrong side of the fabric as you sew the button on the right side.

Thicker fabrics require that you use a button with a shank, or make your own sewn button shank.

· ·

Q **How do I sew a button shank?**

A A button shank allows space between the button and the fabric to which it is attached.

If you need to create a shank, put a toothpick or small crochet hook between the button and the button band to create a space, and begin to sew on the button in the usual way. Before you finish it off, remove your spacer, bring the thread up through the button band, around the loose threads between the button and the band, and back to the wrong side, take a couple of small stitches on the back of the button band, and cut the thread.

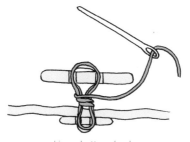

making a button shank

Q Can I put a crocheted border on my knit sweater?

A Absolutely! Crocheted edges can enhance knit garments. Because crocheted borders are firm and flat, they can serve as a good substitute for knitted edgings, which may curl or stretch out of shape. Crocheted buttonholes are usually an improvement over knit ones, as well.

Start with a crochet hook in a size larger than the needle size you used for knitting. For example, if you used a US size 7 (4.5 mm) knitting needle, use a 5.0 mm crochet hook. Follow the instructions above for picking up edge stitches along a crocheted fabric, practicing first on your knit swatch if possible. Crochet stitches usually are wider than their knit cousins, so chances are you won't be picking up one crochet stitch for every knit stitch or row.

CHAPTER 10

The Finish Line

YOU'RE ALMOST FINISHED STITCHING, but you dread the next step? Although finishing may never be one of your favorite tasks, with the right knowledge you may find it becomes less onerous.

All's Well That Ends Well

Q **What is the first step in finishing?**

A Starting out right. An important but often overlooked aspect of finishing starts before you first pick up your hook. Knowing what to expect of your fabric and using good technique throughout make the final finishing steps easier.

Use your washed and blocked swatch to practice borders, buttonholes, and any other finishing details.

SEE ALSO: *Pages 123–25, for working a swatch.*

Q **Too late. I didn't read that part and I've already finished stitching. What do I do now?**

A Once again the answer is: "It depends." The finishing methods you choose depend in part on the yarn, the fabric you have made, and the purpose of the finished item. For instance, if you are making a stuffed toy, you can just stuff it and sew it together with no blocking. If you are making a thread doily, on the other hand, you need to wash, block, and starch it. If you are making a garment, you may need to block the pieces before you sew them together, then add edgings or other finishing touches. No matter what the finishing method, the first step is weaving in ends.

. . . .

Q **How do I *weave in ends*?**

A There is no one right way to weave in ends. Whatever works for you and you are happy with is right. The ends don't have to be invisible from the wrong side, but you don't want them slipping to the front of the work to be seen by all and sundry.

Here's one method that works well on most fabrics: Thread a tapestry needle with the yarn tail. (When beginning and ending a yarn, always leave at least a 6" (15 cm) tail, so you'll have an end to work with.) On the wrong side, run the tip of the tapestry needle through the back of several stitches in one direction, then turn and run it through the back of every other stitch in the other

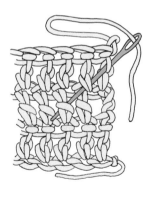

weaving in ends

direction, or through the back of every stitch on the next row in the other direction. You may need to try a variety of ways to get ends to stay put, depending on your yarn and fabric. If you're working with silk, rayon, or other slippery yarns, you need longer tails so that you can weave them diagonally one way and then diagonally in the other direction.

If you have long tails left where you finished a ball and are going to be sewing a seam, you may leave those alone for now. You can either use those ends for seaming, or work the tails into the seam after it is made.

- -

Q Any tips on threading a tapestry needle? I hate the way the yarn always seems to split when I try.

A The easy way? Fold the yarn tail over the needle and pinch it up near the needle. Holding your fingers next to the needle, slide the yarn off the pointed end of the needle and insert the folded end into the needle's eye.

- -

Q What if my ends are too short to weave in?

A You can use a crochet hook or latch hook to draw the ends under other stitches. Next time you make something, be more generous with the ends so that you'll have more to work with.

- -

Q **How do I weave in ends on a chain?**

A This presents a bit more of a problem, since you don't have much there to weave into. With a tapestry needle, go back and forth around the bump on the reverse side of the chain, or try going round and round that bump. Tug the chain a bit before trimming the ends to allow the tails to stretch with the chains. Try different methods to see what works best with your yarn.

Crocheter's Block

Q **What is *blocking?* Do I have to do it?**

A Blocking is the means by which pieces are shaped to their final measurements, using moisture and sometimes heat. It may be compared to ironing seams open in sewing, but it is not ironing!

Blocking sets the stitches and may enhance the drape of the fabric. It can make all the difference between a "homemade" sweater and a "handmade" sweater. Blocking makes it easier to work seams and edges on blocked pieces, and may enable you to make minor size adjustments. But blocking is not the time to correct size problems caused by inaccurate gauge calculations. It's too late for that!

Many crocheted items benefit from a quick dose of steam and some, like doilies, require blocking in order to reach their final shape.

Q What materials do I need in order to block?

A Depending on which blocking method you use, you need rustproof pins; a steamer, steam iron, or plant mister; and water.

Q What kind of work space do I need?

A It needs to be large and flat, so that the pieces lie flat without hanging over the edge. An ironing board works for small pieces, but you often need something bigger.

The work space needs to be able to withstand some abuse, as it is subjected to moisture and/or heat, as well as to being stuck with pins. It also needs to remain undisturbed until the blocking is finished — from a few minutes to a day or more, depending on the circumstances. For example, wet cotton can take days to dry in the humid summer season. (Voice of Experience: Cats love warm, steamy fabric. A door that closes securely is a bonus.)

Q Do I need to buy a special blocking board?

A No, although having a blocking board made especially for the purpose is a great tool if you have the space to store it. These are available from retailers, or you can make your own from a piece of rigid insulation board purchased from your local home improvement center. Be sure to cover the insulation board with colorfast cotton cloth.

Q If I don't have a blocking board, what should I do?

A You can use a spare bed, a carpeted corner of a room, a large sofa cushion, or a piece of foam rubber. Cover it with a waterproof layer, such as an old shower curtain or trash bag, topped by a couple of layers of towels or blankets. Be sure the towels are old so their colors won't bleed onto your work. (Voice of Experience: Count the number of pins you use and be sure to collect them all when you finish. You don't want to share your bed, carpet, or sofa with large straight pins.)

Q Is there more than one way to block?

A You can choose among three basic methods, based on the fiber content of your yarn and your own preference:

▶ **Wet blocking,** for fibers that can tolerate plenty of water

▶ **Cold blocking,** for fibers that can tolerate dampness but not heat

▶ **Steam blocking,** for fibers that can tolerate damp and heat (the quickest method)

Q Which blocking method should I use?

A Look at your yarn label; it may indicate the best blocking method for that yarn. If different fibers have been combined in the same item, choose the method appropriate for the most delicate fiber. Most animal fibers (wool, mohair, alpaca) tolerate steaming. Plant fibers like cotton and linen can be wet blocked. Some man-made fibers can be ruined by too much heat, so wet or cold blocking is best for those. Novelty and metallic yarns may not be suitable for any type of blocking.

Q How does *wet blocking* work?

A Wash or thoroughly wet the pieces, then squeeze out excess water. Do not wring or twist! Place pieces face down on the blocking surface and pat into shape. Use a yardstick to make sure the pieces are the size you want. Check to be sure that each sleeve is blocked to the same dimension. Pin onto the blocking surface at each corner and at approximately 2–3" (5–7.5 cm) intervals along edges.

(Voice of Experience, emphatic: Make sure your pins are rustproof. Rust stains do not come out.) Allow the items to dry. If you are impatient, you can set up a fan to blow over the surface to hasten drying.

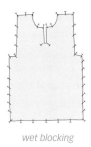

wet blocking

Q **What's the procedure for *cold blocking*?**

A Place the dry pieces on the blocking surface as for wet blocking and pin along each edge. Check your measurements, and make sure that the rustproof pins are close enough together so they don't distort the fabric. Spritz the pieces with clean water until they are damp. Allow them to dry.

Q **How do I *steam block*?**

A Fill a steam iron or steamer with water and use the "steam" setting. Using the dry pieces, measure and pin as for wet blocking. Hold the iron no closer than 1" (2.5 cm) over fabric, and allow steam to work into fabric. Move the iron as needed to cover entire fabric. *Do not press or allow the iron to touch the fabric.* Leave undisturbed until pieces are cool and dry.

What's the recommended way to block three-dimensional pieces?

Wet blocking may be the best bet. Get the pieces damp, then stuff them with rolled-up plastic grocery bags or other waterproof material. If the piece is round, fill it with an inflated balloon. Leave it undisturbed until it is dry. You can put a hat on a wig stand.

....

How do I block a doily?

Doilies, snowflakes, and other lacy thread crochet items sometimes come off the hook looking a bit like a rag, but careful blocking brings out their beauty.

To ensure that your points are symmetrical, prepare a template for the piece by drawing the desired shape on a piece of paper. Cover the paper with plastic wrap or wax paper, and place it on your blocking board. If you are going to starch the piece, do so now. Otherwise, wash or wet the item thoroughly, then pin it onto the template using rustproof pins. You may need to stretch it a bit. Start by pinning opposite sides and the major points, then pin out scallops or any other special shaping. Allow it to dry thoroughly.

You may find it helpful to copy and enlarge the sample doily blocker on the facing page.

....

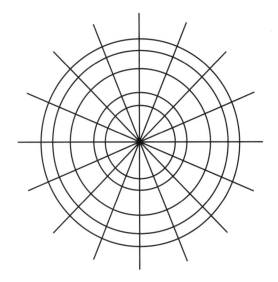

sample doily blocker

Q How do I stiffen thread crochet?

A Whether and how you stiffen your thread crochet item depends on its intended use. Three-dimensional items like baskets may require a permanent hard finish, while doilies may look better with a softer hold. When you select your starch, keep in mind that some turn yellow with age and many are not resistant to moisture.

▶ **Spray starch.** Although spray starch gives a weak hold, it's easy to do and is appropriate when you want to use it to add just a bit of body to a piece. To stiffen with spray starch, prepare a template and pin the item to it to block as described for doilies (or other items) above. Spray on starch when pieces are pinned out but still wet.

▶ **Liquid starches.** For each of the following methods, prepare the mixture, dip piece(s) in mixture to wet thoroughly, and squeeze out excess. Block as described above.

Powdered or liquid starch. Follow mixing directions on the container. You can make the item stiffer, if desired, by using a higher concentration of starch than directed.

Sugar starch. Boil together equal parts sugar and water until syrupy. Allow to cool slightly. This is an old-fashioned method and easy to do, but it may attract ants. In addition, sugar-starched items may wilt in high humidity.

Cornstarch. Mix 6 parts water to 1 part cornstarch and water. Cook over medium heat until thickened. Allow to cool slightly.

Glue. Mix well equal parts white glue and water. As with sugar starch, dampness can be a problem with glue-starched items.

There are several other commercial stiffening products on the market, each with different holding properties. Follow instructions on the container.

Blocking sounds like too much trouble. Do I always have to do it?

No. Some things really are fine without any blocking at all. Some three-dimensional pieces might be difficult to handle, certain fibers may not be suitable for blocking, and very small items such as Christmas ornaments may not need it at all. Some acrylics do best with a simple trip through the washer and dryer. Most natural fibers, garments, and anything that needs to be seamed, however, benefit from a good blocking.

Joining Motifs

My afghan squares aren't all the same size. Is there anything I can do about it?

Oops! If you notice the problem right away, before you finish stitching, check to be sure you are following the instructions correctly and that you didn't accidentally change hook sizes. If the squares are done in different stitch patterns, however, you may have to use a different hook size for each stitch pattern in order for all the squares to come out the same size.

If you notice the problem after you've made all of your squares, maybe you can block them to match. Blocking can sometimes accomplish small size changes, but don't count on brute force and a bit of steam to make a 10" (25 cm) square into a 12" (30 cm) square. Instead, try working an extra round or two on the smaller squares to bring them up to size.

If just a few squares are larger than the others, perhaps you can take out a round or two to bring them into line, or re-stitch the large ones on a smaller hook.

. . . .

Q **How do I join separate motifs?**

A You have a lot of choices here. Your joining method is dependent on the look you want and on the type of stitch you used on the last round of your square. Do you want the join to be part of the overall design, or do you want it to be invisible, or almost so? Stitching the final round of each square in the same color makes invisible joining easier. A single crochet or reverse single crochet join on the right side, on the other hand, makes the join a decorative element.

Experiment with each of the options listed below to determine which one looks best with your project, if specific joining instructions are not given in your published pattern or if you want a different look to your finished project than the original shown in a photo.

No matter which method you use, check from time to time to make sure you are working at the correct tension. The seams should have a similar feel and fluidity to the rest of the fabric.

▶ Wrong sides together, whipstitch through both loops.

▶ Wrong sides together whipstitch through back loops only.

▶ Wrong sides together, slip stitch through both loops.

whipstitching through back loops only

▶ Wrong sides together, slip stitch through back loops only. This is a good choice when the last row of each square is a different color.

▶ Wrong sides together, single crochet through both loops.

▶ Wrong sides together, single crochet through back loops only.

SEE ALSO: *Page 253, for illustration of single crochet join.*

▶ Right sides together, single crochet through both loops.

SEE ALSO: *Pages 252–53, for slip stitch and single crochet joins.*

▶ Use a chain stitch join. This adds a bit of openwork between the squares. (For how to do this, see next question.)

▶ Join motifs as you work.

SEE ALSO: *Page 249, for joining motifs as you work.*

Q How do I work a *chain stitch join*?

A This decorative joining method is usually done on square pieces. Arrange the squares in the desired pattern. Slip stitch (or single crochet) in corner of one square to join yarn, chain 3, then slip stitch (or single crochet) into the

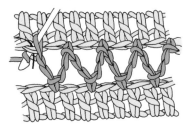

chain stitch join

second or third stitch from the corner of the adjacent square. Continue to alternate slip stitches (or single crochet) and 3-stitch chains back and forth between the squares, skipping one or more stitches between each joining stitch.

....

Q Is it possible to adapt the chain stitch join for a granny square?

A Yes. Slip stitch (or single crochet) into the corner of one granny square, ch 3,

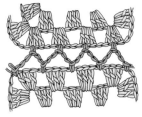

chain stitch join for granny square

stitch into the center stitch of the first dc-3 group on the adjacent square, chain 3, stitch into the ch-1 space of the first square, and so on.

. . . .

Q **How do I join motifs as I work?**

A This method works when the final round of each motif has a lacy or openwork edge. If you are working from a published pattern, the instructions may explain how to join the motifs as you work. If you don't have finishing instructions, look at your motifs and see how they fit together. Draw a diagram so you can see where the motifs touch. Do they meet at certain points only or do they touch along the entire edge?

Complete one motif. On the final round of the next motif, work to the spot where the motifs should touch and insert the hook into the first motif to make a stitch at the spot where they touch (probably a chain space). Continue to work the final round of the second motif, joining to the first motif at appropriate points in the same manner.

Joins in General

Q **How do I assemble my sweater pieces?**

A Sweaters are usually put together in the following order:

1. Sew shoulder seams.
2. Work front and neck borders, and possibly lower edges.
3. Set in sleeves.
4. Sew body and underarm seams.
5. Work lower edge if not already done.

For comfort, you need to use a seaming method that creates little bulk on the inside of the sweater. Experiment to determine the best method for your sweater.

You may slip stitch or whip stitch the shoulder seams from the wrong side. You'll probably want to use mattress stitch to work the side and underarm seams, as it makes a flexible, virtually invisible join. Some people prefer to use slip stitch or single crochet to join all sweater pieces.

. . . .

Q **What is *mattress stitch*?**

A Mattress stitch is done using a tapestry needle and working on the right side of the fabric. After all, that's the side that needs to look good, and so you want to be able to keep an eye on how the seam is shaping up. Working from the right side makes matching stripes or stitch patterns a breeze.

MATTRESS STITCH

1. Hold the pieces to be joined with right sides facing up, side-by-side and parallel to each other. Use a blunt-tip tapestry needle and a length of the same yarn you stitched with. If you have a long tail left over from the foundation chain at one corner, begin with that. If you need to start a new yarn, leave a 6" (15 cm)

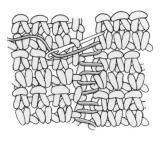

mattress stitch

tail to be woven in later, but don't knot the yarn.

2. Insert the needle vertically under and out a stitch on one piece and then under and out of a stitch exactly opposite on the other piece. Moving up a row on the first piece, stitch under the next stitch on that side, then under the corresponding stitch on the second piece. Do this a couple of more times on each side, then tug gently on the working yarn to pull the two pieces together. Don't pull too hard, just hard enough to get them to sit next to each other.

3. Continue stitching back and forth between the pieces and snugging them together every so often for the length of the seam. When the seaming is complete, weave in the ends of the seaming yarn.

Q How do I handle mattress stitch with various kinds of stitches?

A When you are joining single crochet fabric, you'll probably go into every stitch on each side. If you are working with a double or treble crochet fabric, you may need to put a stitch into the side of each post as well as at the top or bottom of the stitch. When using a fancy or openwork pattern stitch, you'll have to experiment to discover the best place to put your seaming stitches.

....

Q How do I slip stitch pieces together?

A This is done on the wrong side of the fabric. Hold the pieces to be joined with right sides together. Insert the hook all the way through both edge stitches. Yarn over and pull through a loop. *Insert the hook into the next pair of stitches and pull up a loop through both layers of fabric and on through the first loop on hook; repeat from * until the

slip stitch join

entire length is joined. Slip stitch seams can be tight and unforgiving. As you work, stop and examine what you've

done to insure that you have maintained an even tension. If your seam is too tight, you may need to use a larger hook than the one you used on the garment.

. . . .

Q **How do I single crochet pieces together?**

A This is similar to making a slip stitch seam, but you work single crochet instead of slip stitch. The seam is bulkier yet more flexible than a slip stitch seam.

single crochet join

. . . .

Q **Why don't my pieces fit together evenly?**

A Count your rows or stitches to make sure they are the same on each piece to be joined. If not, can you add or remove a row or two? Did your gauge change? Try sewing the pieces from the right side, matching row for row.

You may be able to block them to the same size, or possibly adjust which rows/stitches you are joining a bit when you sew them together to make a better match. (Just a little adjusting here: Don't try to hide a 2" (5 cm) difference, as a buckling seam is sure to give away your secret!)

Zip!

Q **How do I insert a zipper into a sweater?**

A First, choose a zipper appropriate for your garment. Heavy-weight separating zippers are suitable for outer garments like heavy jackets and coats. Medium-weight zippers are meant for cardigans. The length of the zipper should match the length of the opening. Here's how to do it:

INSERTING A ZIPPER

1. Sew the sweater pieces together as far as possible, leaving the zipper for last.

2. Right-side facing, pin one edge of the zipper to the wrong side of the fabric, taking care to keep it in a straight line with the fabric's edge. *To hide the zipper,* make the edges of the crocheted fabric cover the center of the zipper. *To feature the zipper as a design element,* place the center of the zipper a bit further away from the fabric's edge.

3. Baste the zipper in place with sewing thread.

4. Repeat this process on the other side of the zipper, centering the zipper between the fabrics. Check to ensure that the basted-in zipper is straight.

5. On the right side, with sewing thread in the same color as your yarn, back stitch the zipper in place near the edge of the fabric.

6. On the wrong side, whipstitch the outer edges of the zipper to the fabric.

Q What stitch pattern is best for a zipper placket?

A The edge of the crocheted fabric should be finished with a firm, straight border, such as two or three rows of single crochet. A final row of backward single crochet makes a nice decorative edge.

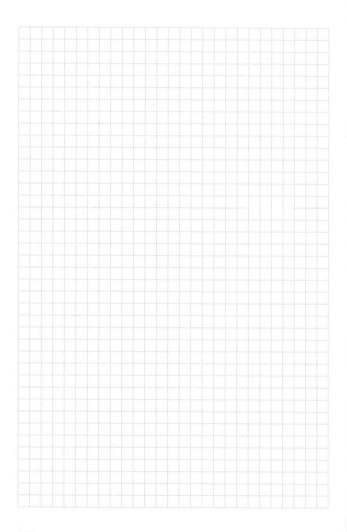

CHAPTER 11

Something (Not Quite) Completely Different

UP TO THIS POINT, we've talked about the basics of crocheting and following patterns. Now it's time to sample some extras that can enhance your newly found knowledge. If you are intrigued by any of these techniques, take time to explore them further using additional resources (see Books, page 305).

Tunisian Crochet

Q What is *Tunisian crochet?*

A Tunisian crochet, also called *afghan stitch*, is a crochet technique worked with a long-handled tool called an afghan hook, which looks like a cross between a knitting needle and a crochet hook. Indeed, Tunisian crochet combines elements of both crochet and knitting. Simple Tunisian crochet stitches are square, making them an ideal base for cross-stitch embellishment.

afghan hook

Q How does Tunisian crochet work?

A Tunisian crochet is made with a combination of forward rows and return rows. Here's how:

TUNISIAN SIMPLE STITCH

1. Base row. With an afghan hook, chain as many stitches as you need for the width of your piece. Insert hook into second chain from hook and pull up a loop as you would for single crochet. Leave that loop on the hook, and pull up another loop in the next chain. Continue on down the chain, pulling up a loop in each chain and leaving it on the hook. Do not turn the work.

2. Return Row. Yo and pull through first loop on hook (the equivalent of a turning chain), *yo, and pull through 2 loops on hook; repeat from * across row.

3. Forward Row. *Insert hook from right to left (left to right for Lefties) under vertical bar of the next-to-last stitch in the previous row and pull up a loop; repeat from * across row. Do not turn the work.

4. Continue working these last two rows for the Tunisian simple pattern, ending with a Return Row.

5. To bind off. Work a slip stitch row as follows: *Insert hook under next vertical bar and pull up a loop, pulling the loop all the way through loop on hook, so that one loop remains on hook; repeat from * across row.

. . . .

Q **Can I work stitch patterns in Tunisian crochet?**

A Absolutely! You can make a fabric that closely resembles knitting, or you can work Tunisian rib, basket weave, bobbles, clusters, and a variety of other stitches. You can increase and decrease.

. . . .

Q **What projects are best suited to Tunisian crochet?**

A Most people associate Tunisian crochet with afghans. (After all, another name for the technique is "afghan stitch"!) Warm garments can be made with afghan stitch, as well. The length of the hook limits the width of the fabric, however, so wide garment pieces and afghans must be stitched separately, then seamed.

Other Kinds of Crochet

Q What is *double-ended crochet?*

A Double-ended crochet is a type of Tunisian crochet worked with a long, double-ended hook. It is usually done with two contrasting colors and makes a thick fabric perfect for afghans, potholders, and so on.

double-ended hook

Q How do I work double-ended crochet?

A There are several different techniques you can use when working double-ended crochet. Here's just one: Using a double-ended hook and two contrasting color yarns, begin by chaining the number of stitches needed for your desired width with Color A.

DOUBLE-ENDED CROCHET

ROW 1: Pick up a loop in each chain as for Tunisian crochet. Drop Color A, but do not cut it.

ROW 2: Turn the work and push it to the other end of the hook. With Color B, work a return row under the vertical bar as for Tunisian crochet. Do not turn.

ROW 3: With Color B, work a Forward Row of Tunisian crochet. You'll be working under the vertical bar formed by Color A. Count to see that you've maintained the same number of stitches. Drop Color B.

ROW 4: Turn the work and push it to the other end of the hook. With Color A, work a Return Row of Tunisian crochet.

ROW 5: With Color A, work a Forward Row of Tunisian crochet, working under the vertical bars formed by Color B. Count your stitches again.

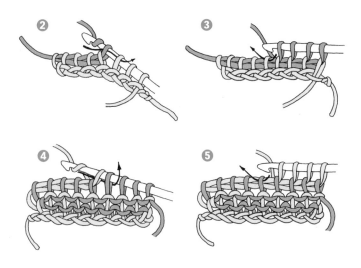

Repeat Rows 2–5 until desired length. Finish off with a Tunisian bind-off.

Note: As you finish each pair of rows, the yarn you need to pick up will be waiting for you at the beginning of the row. There are variations of this simple double-ended stitch. Buy a published pattern and experiment!

Q How can I keep track of where I am in double-ended crochet?

A If you are lost, take a look at where you are, what's on your hook, and what needs to happen next. You'll see that you are working two rows of each color. The first row of each color starts when the hook is full of stitches in the contrasting color, and ends with just a single stitch on the hook. The second row of each color loads up the hook again with stitches. Turn the hook at the end of every other row, when it is full of stitches and a new color is about to begin.

Q What is *thread crochet?*

A Thread crochet is crochet made with very smooth yarn, called thread. The thread is most commonly made of cotton, although there are silk and linen threads as well. The thread may be fine, requiring a small steel hook. Thread crochet is used to make lace and filet stitch patterns.

Q What is *Irish crochet?*

A Irish crochet is a type of thread crochet that results in beautiful three-dimensional lace. It was developed in Ireland to mimic the more expensive European needle laces. Floral motifs are worked individually, then joined with a mesh or filling stitch to form the lace fabric. Traditionally, stitches in the motifs were worked over a cord to pad and add dimension to the stitches. Traditional Irish crochet is not currently in fashion, although modern crochet borrows certain techniques and motifs from Irish crochet, and we tend to call any thread crochet involving flowers "Irish crochet." Thread flower and leaf motifs on mesh backgrounds are a bow to the traditional Irish techniques.

Q What is *filet crochet?*

A Filet crochet is another type of thread crochet. In filet crochet, double crochet and chain stitches are arranged to form a grid or *ground* of blocks and spaces. Filet crochet often depicts letters and pictures. When you work a pattern, the pictures and motifs are presented as graphs. The example shown here is a simplified version

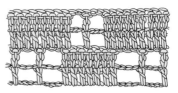

filet crochet

of a technique that often results in an intricate and beautifully lacy fabric.

. . . .

Q **What kind of hook and thread should I use for filet crochet?**

A You can use any size thread you like; the size of the thread will determine the size of the grid. The smaller the thread/grid, the more detail you can incorporate into your design. Use an appropriate-sized hook for your chosen thread.

. . . .

Q **How do I read a filet crochet graph?**

A Each square in a filet crochet chart represents either a *block* that is filled with double crochets or a *space* that is created by chain stitches. The block can be made up of either three, four, or five double crochet stitches. The space is made by either one, two, or three chains and a double crochet. When working

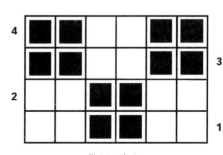

filet crochet

a block over a space, you work the stitches into the chain space rather than into the chain stitches.

Start at the bottom right-hand corner of the chart. (Lefties should start at the bottom left, and reverse the following directions.) Follow the first row from right to left; follow the second row from left to right. It may be easier to under-stand this if you pick up the yarn and hook and try it out,

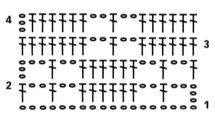

symbol crochet

using the sample filet crochet chart on page 265. Each dark-ened square represents three double crochet stitches, and each white square represents a chain 2 and a double crochet. In addition, there is a double crochet at the end of the row to balance the pattern.

To determine the number of stitches you need for the foundation chain, count the number of squares across the bottom row. Multiply that number by three, then add one. Next, note whether the beginning square of the first row is a block or a space. If it's a block, add chain 3 to your starting chain to count as the first dc of the block. If the first square is a space, add chain 5 to your starting chain to count as a ch-3 dc plus a ch-2 mesh.

For example: (6 x 3) +1 = 19

19 + 5 = 24 sts for starting chain on filet chart.

Here is the text version of the first three rows of the sample chart:

ROW 1: Dc in 9th ch from hook, skip 2 ch, dc in next ch, *dc in next 6 ch, (skip 2 ch, dc in next ch) twice; repeat from * across, turn.

ROW 2: Ch 5 (counts as dc plus ch-2), dc in next dc, ch 2, dc in next dc, *dc in next 6 dc, (ch 2, dc in next dc) twice; repeat from * across, ending last repeat with a dc in top of turning chain, turn.

ROW 3: Ch 3, (2 dc in ch-2 sp, dc in next dc) twice, *(skip 2 dc, dc in next dc) twice, (2 dc in chain space, dc in next dc) twice; repeat from *, ending last repeat with a dc in top of turning chain, turn.

. . . .

Q **What is *free-form crochet*?**

A It's fun! Free-form crochet is a completely pattern-free way of crocheting. Indeed, to do it properly, you *can't* have a plan. You use scraps of yarn and a variety of stitch patterns and shapes to paint a textural fabric. Hard to explain, but easy to do!

Using a yard or two of yarn, crochet a little piece in any shape, in any stitch pattern that suits you. Increase and decrease willy-nilly to create a free-form shape. We're not talking squares here, but little pieces that move. Do only a few rows/rounds, then end off the first yarn. Add on to the first piece with other yarns in your choice of coordinating colors, picking up stitches from the edge of the existing piece. Your free-form motif can be any size or shape. If you are trying to make a particular shape (such as for a purse or a vest), you may have to crochet a few extra pieces to fit your puzzle, but that's the only time you should have to plan.

This is a technique that unleashes your artistic side! Mix a variety of yarns, weights, and colors to create a unique fabric.

Q **What do crocheters do with their free-form pieces?**

A You can do anything you chose. Use tiny free-form shapes as brooches or embellishments. Use larger free-form pieces to make vests, coats, afghans, pillows, or wall hangings. If you are shaping a garment, use newsprint to make a full-sized template of each garment piece you need. Make smaller free-form pieces [about 6–8 square inches (15–20 square cm) each] and place them on your template, then fill in the spaces as necessary to create your desired shape.

Q **Is there anything I should be cautious about with free-form crochet?**

A It can be addictive! You may not want to go back to traditional crocheting when you get a taste of free-form fun.

Q My first tries at free-form crochet are very rippled. How can I get them to lay flat?

A Are you sure you want them to be flat? Free-form crochet is just that. Three-dimensionality, including bumps and ripples, can be part of the beauty of the design. However, if you don't like the results you are getting, review the guidelines in Chapter 6 about making round motifs lie flat, and those in Chapter 10 about making flat edges.

Q Can I combine crochet with knit?

A Great idea! There are some items that are better knitted than crocheted — and vice versa. Three-dimensional items are easier to crochet than to knit. Knitted fabric's flexibility means that it may be better suited for sweaters and garments, but stockinette stitch tends to curl. However, crochet is less flexible and more likely to lie flat. You might want to add crocheted edging onto your knitted sweaters, or knitted cuffs onto your crocheted sweater. Use your imagination and you'll think of dozens of other ways to combine the two.

Baubles and Beads

Q **How do I add beads to my crochet?**

A There are several different beading techniques for crochet — enough for another book or two! Here is a method I like:

The first step is to string the beads onto your yarn before you begin to crochet. You have to plan ahead to know how many beads you need. The beads wait near your yarn ball until you're ready for them. When you work them in, they show on the back side of the stitch; your beading row is always a wrong side row so that they will appear on the right side of the fabric.

▶ **For single crochet.** Work to the spot where you want to insert a bead; insert hook into stitch and pull up a loop, pull a bead up so that it is next to the hook, then yarn over and pull through both loops on hook. You can also pull up beads *between* single crochet stitches.

beading with single crochet

beading between single crochet

▶ **For double crochet.** You can pull up the bead at one of two places, either after the first "yarnover, insert hook and pull up loop," or following that, after the "yarnover and pull through two loops on hook."

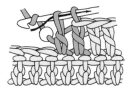

beading with double crochet

You can also make loops of beads for fringe, by pulling up many beads together and allowing them to hang from the front of the fabric before working the next stitch.

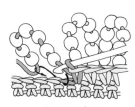

beads as fringe

Q **My beads don't show. What did I do wrong?**

A You probably worked them in on a right-side row. Be sure to work them in on wrong-side rows only. If your yarn is fuzzy or highly textured, the beads may be hidden by the yarn. Try larger beads or a different yarn. If you are following a pattern, check the instructions to make sure you have followed them correctly.

Q How do I make yarn *fringe*?

A Cut lengths of yarn twice the length you want your finished fringe to be, plus 1 or 2 inches (2.5–5 cm). You need the extra length to allow for the knot and for a bit to be trimmed off. Holding 3 or more strands together, fold them in half to form a loop. Insert a crochet hook from the wrong side to the right side of the edge of the fabric and pull through the loop made by the folded strands. Draw the ends of the fringe through the loop and tug gently to tighten the knot.

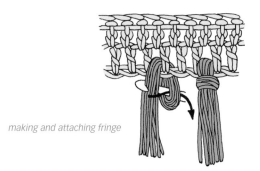

making and attaching fringe

Q My fringe looks pitiful. What's wrong?

A Don't be stingy with your yarn! Good fringe takes lots of yarn. Use lengths that are long enough to be in proportion to your crocheted item, use enough strands in each bundle, and place the bundles close enough together to give a luxurious look. Thin yarn can make thin fringe; use lots of yarn or use a different yarn for the fringe.

Some yarns don't hold up well for fringe. Test your yarn's hardiness and suitability for fringe by holding a few strands together and running your hands down past the ends of the yarn, squeezing a bit as you do so. Do this several times. Now shake the ends. Are they starting to look ragged? Did you harvest large bits of fuzz when you ran your hand over the yarn? If so, you may want to choose another yarn for fringing, or to omit the fringe altogether.

- -

Q Is it "pompom" or "pompon"?

A Either one.

- -

Q How do I make a *pompom*?

A Start with either a commercial pompom maker or cut out two doughnut-shaped cardboard disks for a homemade pompom maker. The pompom will be slightly smaller than the outside diameter of your disks, so you can make any size you wish.

MAKING A POMPOM

1. Holding the disks together, wrap yarn through the center and around the outside of both pieces until you can't fit any more yarn through the center hole — or until you can't stand wrapping any more! (Voice of Experience: You'll be tired of this process long before you are finished, but keep wrapping.)

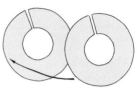

2. Using sharp scissors and holding the center of the pompom maker carefully, cut along the outer edge of the disks, making sure the bottom blade of the scissors is between the two disks, as if you were cutting along the groove of a yo-yo. Don't separate the disks yet!

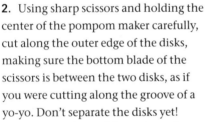

3. Take a 10" (25 cm) long piece of yarn, and wrap it tightly around the center of the pompom bundle, between the disks. Tie a knot, leaving enough of a tail on each end to sew the pompom onto the item you've crocheted.

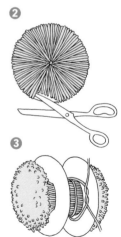

4. Fluff pompom with your fingers, and trim it, if necessary.

How do I make a *tassel*?

Tassels are easier than pompoms!

MAKING A TASSEL

Cut a piece of strong cardboard ½ to 1" (1.25–2.5 cm) longer than the desired length of your tassel. (If you can find a book about the right size, use that as your template.) Next, cut a 4" to 7" (10–17.5 cm) length of yarn and place it across the top of the template. This will be the hanging loop.

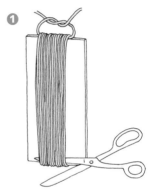

1. Wrap yarn lengthwise around the template as many times as you need to get the desired thickness. Tie the hanging loop securely around the top of the tassel. Cut yarn at base of cardboard.

2. Slide the wraps and hanging loop carefully off the template.

3. Cut an additional length of yarn about 2½ times the length of the tassel. Wrap this piece tightly around all the strands, ¼" to 1" (.5–2.5 cm) from the hanging loop. Secure the ends of the wrapping yarn by threading them under the wraps and down through the center of the tassel. Trim the ends.

· ·

Q How do I make a *twisted cord*?

A Also known as a *monk's cord,* this popular cord is simple for even non-crocheters.

MAKING MONK'S CORD

1. Cut three or more strands of yarn at least 3 times the desired finished length. Place an overhand knot at each end of the bundle of yarn. Put a crochet hook or pencil into one end to act as a handle. Slip the other end over a hook or doorknob. (Voice of Experience: Even better — get someone to help you hold one end. Kids love to do this!)

2. Using the "handle," twist the yarn until it is tight. You may have to move a little closer to the

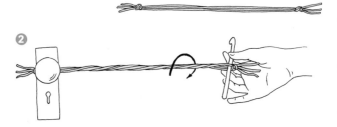

stationary end as you twist, but keep some tension on it and hold on! As it twists, it tends to jump out of your hands and kink up.

3. Pinch the yarn at the halfway point and bring the knotted ends together, allowing the cord to twist on itself.

4. Carefully untie the knots and re-tie all the strands together.

If you like, you can make tassels at each end of the cord by tying a knot several inches from each end and allowing the ends to unravel.

Tender Care

Q How do I clean my finished piece?

A Now that you've spent all that time making your gorgeous crocheted project, you'll want it to last a long time. When you made your swatch, you read the care instructions on the yarn label, and then washed and blocked your swatch if it was appropriate for the fiber content, so you know what to expect.

Before you launder your handiwork, take a look to see that buttons and any embellishments are secure, and that no ends are coming loose. (Voice of Experience: Some buttons cannot be laundered; others cannot be dry-cleaned. You may need to remove these before washing or dry cleaning.)

If you can machine-wash and -dry your item, by all means do so. Use the gentle cycle and low heat. Many machine-washable yarns need to be machine-dried as well to regain their elasticity.

Hand wash fabrics by using tepid water and a small amount of gentle soap or detergent. Put the item into the sudsy water and gently squeeze the lather through the fabric. Rinse well. Squeeze out excess water gently. Do not wring or twist! Now you have two options for removing excess water:

▶ Pick up the wet item carefully, supporting its weight, and lay it flat between two clean towels. Roll the item and towels together, and squeeze to blot out the excess water.

▶ Put the wet item into the washing machine, and run a gentle spin cycle for a few moments. Finish by laying the piece flat to dry.

Dry cleaning is a good option for novelty yarns and others labeled "dry clean only." (Voice of Experience: Some yarns labeled "dry clean" can be carefully hand washed. If you suspect yours can be hand washed, try washing a swatch.)

Q How should I store crocheted items?

A Clean them first; body oils attract dirt that appears like magic when items are put away and makes wool more attractive to moths. Fold crocheted items, if possible, and store them in a dark, dust-proof container. If the item is going to be stored for a long time, refold it from time to time to avoid permanent creases that might weaken the fabric. Use a moth repellent for animal fibers or blends.

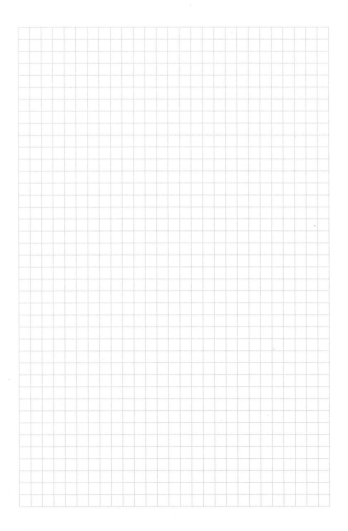

Resources

Standard Crochet Abbreviations

SYMBOL	ABBREVIATION	TERM/EXPLANATION
	( ) OR [ ] OR { }	Work instructions within parentheses/brackets as many times as directed
	*	Repeat instructions following asterisk as many times as directed
	**	Repeat instructions between asterisks as many times as directed, or repeat directions from a certain point
	alt	alternate/alternating Every other
	beg	begin, beginning
	bet	between
	BL	back loop(s) Loop away from you at top of stitch
	bo	bobble
)	BP	back post
Ŧ	BPdc	back post double crochet
Ƈ	BPsc	back post single crochet
Ŧ	BPtr	back post triple crochet
	CA	color A

SYMBOL	ABBREVIATION	TERM/EXPLANATION
	CB	color B
	CC	contrasting color
⬭ AND 0	ch(s)	chain stitch, chain(s) Starting with sl st on hook, hook working yarn and pull through
	ch-sp	chain space
	CL	cluster
	cm	centimeter
	cont	continue
⊤	dc	double crochet Yarn over, insert hook into the stitch, yarn over. Pull yarn through stitch. (Yarn over and pull through 2 loops) twice.
⋏	dc2tog	Double crochet two together
	dec	decrease, decreasing
	FL	front loop(s) Loop nearest you at the top of stitch
	foll	follow, follows, following
ʅ	FP	front post
⊤ʅ	FPdc	front post double crochet

SYMBOL	ABBREVIATION	TERM/EXPLANATION
ろ	FPsc	front post single crochet
₮ろ	FPtr	front post triple crochet
	g OR gm	gram
T	hdc	half double crochet Yarn over, insert hook into the stitch, yarn over. Pull yarn through stitch. Yarn over and pull through all 3 loops.
	hk	hook
	in(s)	inch(es)
	inc	increase, increasing
	jn	join Usually, slip stitch to first stitch of round
	LH	left hand
	lp(s)	loop(s)
	m	meter(s)
	MB	make bobble
	MC	main color
	meas	measure
	mm(s)	millimeter(s)
	Mult	multiple

SYMBOL	ABBREVIATION	TERM/EXPLANATION
	oz	ounce(s)
	p	picot
	patt OR pat(s)	pattern(s)
	pc	popcorn
	pm	place marker
	prev	previous
	rem	remain, remains, remaining
	rep	repeat(s)
	RH	right hand
	rnd(s)	round(s)
	RS	right side
+ OR **✕**	sc	single crochet Insert hook into the stitch, yarn over. Pull yarn through stitch. Yarn over and pull through 2 loops on hook.
⋊⋉	sc2tog	single crochet 2 together (Insert hook into next stitch and pull through loop) twice, yarn over and pull through all 3 loops on hook
	sk	skip

SYMBOL	ABBREVIATION	TERM/EXPLANATION
	sl	slip
● OR ▬	Sl st	slip stitch Insert hook into stitch, yarn over. Pull yarn through both the stitch and the loop on the hook.
	sp(s)	space(s)
	st(s)	stitch(es)
	tbl	through back loop
	tch OR t-ch	turning chain
	tog	together
⟊	tr	triple crochet, treble crochet Yarn over twice, insert hook into the stitch, yarn over again and pull through stitch. (Yarn over and pull through 2 loops) 3 times.
⟊	trtr	triple treble crochet
	WS	wrong side
	yd(s)	yard(s)
	yoh	yarn over hook same as yarn over
	yo	yarn over

Common Crochet Terms and Phrases

THIS PHRASE	MEANS
Above markers	Measure from where markers were placed
At the same time	You are going to be doing two things at once. For example, neckline and shoulder shaping often occur at the same time.
Attach/join new yarn	Begin working with a separate ball of yarn, either the same color or a different color.
Back, Left Front, Right Front, Left Shoulder, etc.	These are the names of sweater pieces as they are worn. The left shoulder is the part that will be on the wearer's left shoulder. If you have trouble remembering which piece you are working on, hold it up to your body and see which way it fits. *Hint:* Sweater piece names are usually captalized.
Back, front	Beginning with lowercase letters, *back* and *front* usually mean the work as you hold it. The back of the stitch is the side away from you; the front is the side closest to you.

THIS PHRASE	MEANS
Ball band/yarn band	The identifying label on each ball or skein of yarn. It contains information on fiber content, weight, yardage, care instructions, and suggested hook sizes.
Block	Blocking is a very important step in making your garments look professional, and it can solve a multitude of problems. See the index for other articles in this book to learn more about blocking.
Body of sweater is worked in one piece to underarm	Just what it says. You start with enough stitches for the front and back of the sweater at the same time, and work it as one piece until you divide for the armhole openings.
Continue in this manner	Keep on doing whatever you've been doing: increasing, decreasing, working in stitch pattern, whatever the preceding instructions have been.
Ease	The difference between the wearer's body measurement and the finished sweater measurement. Ease is necessary for a good fit, but it varies according to the style of sweater.

THIS PHRASE	MEANS
End off/fasten off	After the last stitch is worked, pull working yarn through last stitch to secure it.
End with WS row (or RS row)	The last row that you work is a SW row (or RS row).
Finished measurements	The measurements of the project after blocking and seaming.
Join	Connect end of one round with beginning of same round, usually with a slip stitch.
Keeping to pattern, keeping in est. pattern	While doing whatever shaping is about to be described, keep working the stitch pattern as you have been, making adjustments for a change in stitch count so that the pattern stitch remains uninterrupted.
Or size needed to obtain gauge	Change hook sizes until you get the gauge called for in the pattern. If your first attempt results in too many stitches per inch, increase your hook size. If you get too few stitches per inch, decrease your hook size.
Post	Vertical part of a stitch

THIS PHRASE	MEANS
Pull up a loop	Wrap yarn around hook and pull it through fabric. This term is usually preceded by "insert hook into stitch/fabric/etc and . . ."
Reverse shaping OR reversing shaping	You are probably working a cardigan front and have worked one side. On the other side, you need to work the neckline and armhole shaping on the opposite side from the piece you just worked.
Right Side, Wrong Side	These are the names for the "public" and "private" sides of a piece.
RS facing/WS facing	The side that you are about to work is the right side (or wrong side) of the fabric
Schematic	A graphic representation of a finished project, showing finished dimensions.
Selvage st OR selvedge st	A stitch at the beginning/end of a row that will be used for seaming or other finishing. It is not part of the pattern stitch. Not all patterns contain selvage stitches, and many that do contain them do not identify them as such.

THIS PHRASE	MEANS
Sizes: S (M,L,XL) [S(M,L,XL)	Patterns usually give several sets of measurements. The first set may be for children and the second set for adults, or the first for women and the second for men; the pattern instructions explain. Determine which size you want to make and circle or otherwise mark it throughout the pattern.
Stitch multiple	The number of stitches used to complete a repeat of a pattern. For example, a stitch multiple of 8 plus 3 would mean that the pattern is worked on a multiple of 8 stitches, plus 3 extra/selvage stitches. Thus, it could be worked over 19 sts, 27 sts, 35 sts, and so on.
Swatch	A small piece of stitching used to determine gauge, fabric hand, washing results, finishing techniques. Swatches are crucial in almost every project. They can tell you much more than just what your gauge is going to be. Please take time to learn to do them well.
Tapestry needle	A large, blunt-tip yarn needle

Standard Body Measurements & Sizing

Reprinted from *Standards & Guidelines for Crochet and Knitting*, (April 2003), with permission of the Craft Yarn Council of America.

Most crochet pattern instructions provide general sizing information, such as the chest or bust measurements of a completed garment. Many patterns also include detailed schematics or show specific garment measurements (bust/ chest, neckline, back, waist, sleeve length, etc.) in all the different pattern sizes. To insure proper fit, always review all of the sizing information provided in a pattern before you begin.

Following are several sizing charts. These charts show Chest, Center Back, Neck-to-Cuff, Back Waist Length, Cross Back, and Sleeve Length actual body measurements for babies, children, women, and men. These measurements are given in both inches and centimeters.

When sizing sweaters, the fit is based on actual chest/bust measurements, plus ease (additional inches or centimeters). The first chart entitled "Fit" recommends the amount of ease to add to body measurements if you prefer a close-fitting garment, an oversized garment, or something in-between.

The next charts provide average length for children's, women's, and men's garments.

Both Fit and Length charts are simply guidelines. For individual body differences, changes can be made in body and sleeve lengths when appropriate. However, consideration must be given to the project pattern. Certain sizing changes may alter the appearance of the garment.

HOW TO MEASURE

CHEST/BUST. Measure around the fullest part of the chest/bust. Do not draw the tape too tightly.

CENTER BACK NECK-TO-CUFF. With arm slightly bent, measure from back base of neck across shoulder around bend of elbow to wrist.

BACK WAIST LENGTH. Measure form the most prominent bone at the base of the neck to the natural waistline.

CROSS BACK. Measure form shoulder to shoulder.

Sleeve Length. With arm slightly bent, measure from armpit to cuff.

FIT

VERY-CLOSE FITTING: Actual chest/bust measurement or less

CLOSE-FITTING: 1–2" (2.5–5 cm)

STANDARD-FITTING: 2–4" (5–10 cm)

LOOSE-FITTING: 4–6" (10–15 cm)

OVERSIZED: 6" (15 cm) or more

LENGTH FOR CHILDREN

WAIST LENGTH: Actual body measurement

HIP LENGTH: 2" (5 cm) down from waist

TUNIC LENGTH: 6" (15 cm) down from waist

LENGTH FOR WOMEN

WAIST LENGTH: Actual body measurement

HIP LENGTH: 6" (15 cm) down from waist

TUNIC LENGTH: 11" (28 cm) down from waist

LENGTH FOR MEN

Men's length usually varies only 1–2" (2.5–5 cm) from the actual "back hip length" measurement *(see chart on page 297)*

Baby's size		3 mo.	6 mo.	12 mo.	18 mo.	24 mo.
Chest	in.	16	17	18	19	20
	cm	40.5	43	45.5	48	50.5
Center Back	in.	10½	11½	12½	14	18
Neck-to-Cuff	cm	26.5	29	31.5	35.5	45.5
Back Waist	in.	6	7	7½	8	8½
Length	cm	15.5	17.5	19	20.5	21.5
Cross Back	in.	7¼	7¾	8¼	8½	8¾
(Shoulder to	cm	18. 5	19.5	21	21. 5	22
shoulder)						
Sleeve Length	in.	6	6½	7½	8	8½
to Underarm	cm	15.5	16.5	19	20.5	21.5

Child's size		2	4	6	8	10
Chest	in.	21	23	25	26½	28
	cm	53	58.5	63.5	67	71
Center Back	in.	18	19½	20½	22	24
Neck-to-Cuff	cm	45.5	49.5	52	56	61
Back Waist	in.	8½	9½	10½	12½	14
Length	cm	21.5	24	26.5	31.5	35.5
Cross Back	in.	9¼	9¾	10¼	10¾	11¼
(Shoulder to	cm	23.5	25	26	27	28.5
shoulder)						
Sleeve Length	in.	8½	10½	11½	12½	13½
to Underarm	cm	21.5	26.5	29	31.5	34.5

Child's (cont.)		12	14	16
Chest (in.)	in.	30	31½	32½
	cm	76	80	82.5
Center Back	in.	26	27	28
Neck-to-Cuff	cm	66	68.5	71
Back Waist	in.	15	15½	16
Length	cm	38	39.5	40.5
Cross Back	in.	12	12¼	13
(Shoulder to	cm	30.5	31	33
Shoulder)				
Sleeve Length	in.	15	16	16½
to Underarm	cm	38	40.5	42

Woman's size		X-Small	Small	Medium	Large
Bust	in.	28–30	32–34	36–38	40–42
	cm	71–76	81–86	91.5–96.5	101.5–106.5
Center Back	in.	27–27½	28–28½	29–29½	30–30½
Neck-to-Cuff	cm	68.5–70	71–72.5	73.5–75	76–77.5
Back Waist	in.	16½	17	17¼	17½
Length	cm	42	43	43.5	44.5
Cross Back	in.	14–14½	14½ –15	16–16½	17–17½
(Shoulder to	cm	35.5–37	37–38	40.5–42	43–44.5
Shoulder)					
Sleeve Length	in.	16½	17	17	17½
to Underarm	cm	42	43	43	44.5

Woman's *(cont.)*		1X	2X	3X	4X	5X
Bust	in.	44–46	48–50	52–54	56–58	60–62
	cm	*111.5–117*	*122–127*	*132–137*	*142–147*	*152–158*
Center Back	in.	31–31½	31½–32	32½–33	32½–33	33–33½
Neck-to-Cuff	*cm*	*78.5–80*	*80–81.5*	*82.5–84*	*82.5–84*	*84–85*
Back Waist	in.	17¾	18	18	18½	18½
Length	*cm*	*45*	*45.5*	*45.5*	*47*	*47*
Cross Back	in.	17½	18	18	18½	18½
(Shoulder to	*cm*	*44.5*	*45.5*	*45.5*	*47*	*47*
Shoulder)						
Sleeve Length	in.	17½	18	18	18½	18½
to Underarm	*cm*	*44.5*	*45.5*	*45.5*	*47*	*47*

Man's size		Small	Medium	Large	X-Large	XX-Large
Chest	in.	34–36	38–40	42–44	46–48	50–52
	cm	*86–91.5*	*96.5–101.5*	*106.5–111.5*	*116.5–122*	*127–132*
Center Back	in.	32–32½	33–33½	34–34½	35–35½	36–36½
Neck-to-Cuff	*cm*	*81–82.5*	*83.5–85*	*86.5–87.5*	*89–90*	*91.5–92.5*
Back Hip	in.	25–25½	26½–26½	27–27½	27½–27¾	28–28½
Length	*cm*	*63.5–64.5*	*67.5–68*	*68.5–69*	*69.5–70.5*	*71–72.5*
Cross Back	in.	15½–16	16½–17	17½–18	18–18½	18½–19
(Shoulder to	*cm*	*39.5–40.5*	*42–43*	*44.5–45.5*	*45.5–47*	*47–48*
Shoulder)						
Sleeve Length	in.	18	18½	19½	20	20½
to Underarm	*cm*	*45.5*	*47*	*49.5*	*50.5*	*52*

Suggested Sizes for Accessories and Household Items

The following measurements give you a starting point for designing your own accessories and household items.
Note: All sizes are given in inches

AFGHANS come in all sizes and shapes. Here are a few typical sizes, but feel free to experiment with other sizes. If you have big folks in your family, you may want to make larger afghans to cover those long legs and big feet! Note: Afghans measurements usually exclude fringe.	39 x 60 40 x 56–60 43 x 60 45 x 65 48 x 60 46 x 68 50 x 64
LAP RUGS and **THROWS** are somewhat smaller than afghans but again, they can be any size that works for you. Throw-size blankets are a good size for kids.	27 x 34–36 30 x 30 37 x 50 45 x 45
BABY BLANKETS are smaller still. Make items for premies even smaller, about 27–30" square.	**BABY BLANKET:** 25 x 32, 32–36" square 32 x 40 **CRIB BLANKET:** 36 x 54, 40 x 60

PILLOWS may be made to fit purchased pillow forms. Typical pillow form sizes are listed at right.

12–30" square, in 2" increments
6–7 x 14 (neckroll)
12, 14, 16" circles
26" square (Euro)
27" or larger (floor pillows)

FASHION SCARVES can be very skinny (3" wide), although most are 4–6" wide. They can be as short or long as you choose, depending on your taste and how much yarn you have.

WARM SCARVES are another matter and need to be long enough to wrap comfortably around the neck and tie or tuck into a coat. Width is important — too wide and it's hard to wear, too narrow and it's not warm enough. For adults, 7–9" wide by 58–72" long is usually good. Children need narrower, shorter scarves, about 6–7" wide by 45–50" long.

SHAWLS and **STOLES** are about 20" wide by 72–80" long, depending on the height of the wearer. Triangular shawls need to be wide enough to stay wrapped around the shoulders. This depends on the size of the wearer, but may be 62–80" wide across the hypotenuse. The length from center-back to tip is usually in the range of 32–40" inches.

POTHOLDERS are usually about 7" square; dishcloths and washcloths about 9" square. Placemats are 12" x 16–18".

Yarn Care Symbols

Wash		Do not tumble dry		
Hand wash		Iron		
Do not wash		Iron, high heat		
Bleach		Iron, medium heat		
Do not bleach		Iron, low heat		
Tumble dry, normal		Do not iron		
Tumble dry, delicate		Gentle wash		
Line dry		Dry clean		
Do not dry		Do not dry clean		

To Learn More

Despite the promise on the cover, I do realize that I have not answered every question you'll ever have. It would take more than one small book to do that! However, there are many places you can go to learn more about crochet. Visit your local yarn shop, join a local knitting group and the national guild, look for books and magazines at bookstores, and search the Internet. Sign up for knitting classes at your yarn shop, through your recreation department, or at knitting conferences and retreats.

WEB SITES

The Internet has a wealth of information for crocheters. Type in "crochet" on a search engine, and you'll get literally millions of hits! Because Web sites appear and disappear with lightning speed, there's no way to list all of the good ones, but here's a list of sites to get you started:

Crochet Guild of America, *www.crochet.org*. This site has a "how to crochet" section for both left- and right-handers, including a special section on "How to Teach a Child to Crochet." Don't miss the extensive links page.

Learn to Knit & Crochet, *www.learntocrochet.com,* is a Web site of the Craft Yarn Council of America that has how-to illustrations and appealing projects.

YarnStandards.com, *www.yarnstandards.com,* is another CYCA Web site, and it provides the Standards & Guidelines for Crochet and Knitting described in this book.

Crochet at About.com, *www.crochet.about.com.* You could spend all day clicking the links from this site. You'll find free patterns, product reviews yarn sources, beginner to advanced techniques, stitch dictionaries and charts. Even the advertising serves as a resource!

Annie's Attic, *www.stitchguide.com.* Explanations and illustrations of the crochet basics, plus more advanced techniques, all with a bonus -you can watch a video of each stitch as it is made. View clear close-up shots of hands, hook, and yarn, repeating the stitch over and over as many times as you need to understand and learn the technique. Oh, the wonders of technology!

wiseNeedle, *www.wiseneedle.com.* Here, you'll find a treasury of information on yarns, both new and discontinued. Read reviews of the yarns written by real knitters and crocheters, or add your own review. Search yarns by manufacturer, fiber content, weight or yarn name.

INTERNET GROUPS

Tap into the internet for your own online support group. You'll find other crocheters willing to chat about their favorite hobby at all times of the day or night. Many websites host live chats with other crocheters. (If you are past a certain age, ask a friendly teen how to participate in a chat.) You'll also find forums, bulletin-board-type discussion groups where you can post your questions and read responses from others.

List-serves are an excellent way to learn and share with other crocheters. Search www.groups.yahoo.com to find a crochet list-serve that suits your interests. You'll find technically oriented on-topic lists, or more chatty "tell me about your life while we stitch together" lists.

LOCAL RESOURCES

At your local yarn shop or craft store, you may find experienced crocheters willing to answer your questions. Don't just limit yourself to the employees! Talk to other customers; you might be surprised at the level of expertise you find. Ask if there are any crochet guilds in your area, or start your own, meeting at a coffee shop or community center. Members can take turns learning new skills and teaching each other. If you don't know of local yarn shops, look under "Yarn" in the Yellow Pages.

CLASSES

Your local library, recreation center, or community college might offer crochet classes, or you can take advantage of classes at yarn shops and craft stores. You might find someone willing to come to you for customized private instruction. There are also professional crochet teachers willing to come teach workshops in your community. Did you know that there are national crochet conventions, where people from around the country gather to share ideas and learn new techniques?

THE CROCHET GUILD OF AMERICA (CGOA)

CGOA offers a variety of learning resources. They sponsor an annual crochet conference, publish an e-mail newsletter, and offer correspondence courses in basic stitches and thread crochet. Throughout the courses, you prepare a portfolio of swatches and answer questions based on the swatches. Your work is evaluated by a CGOA judge, who may make suggestions of ways to improve your work.

MAGAZINES

Check your newsstand for the many crochet magazines currently available. One of particular interest is Crochet! This full-size color magazines contains contemporary projects and how-to articles, and serves as the official magazine of The Crochet Guild of America.

BOOKS

There are thousands of pattern books for crochet, and dozens of how-to books in print. You can learn a lot from pattern books — just choose projects that use techniques you've never tried before. Follow the instructions, and *voila!,* you've learned a new technique. Stitch dictionaries are also fun for the budding designer. Here are some reference books I find useful:

Blackwell, Liz, *A Treasury of Crochet Patterns* (Charles Scriber's Sons, 1971)

Brown, Nancy, *The Crocheter's Companion* (Interweave Press, 2002)

Chin, Lily, *Knit & Crochet with Bead* (Interweave Press, 2004)

Cosh, Sylvia, and James Walters, *The Crochet Workbook* (St. Martin's Griffin, 1989)

Eaton, Jan, 200 *Crochet Blocks for Blankets, Throws and Afghans* (Interweave Press, 2004)

Gibson-Roberts, Priscilla, *Knitting in the Old Way* (Nomad Press, 2004)

Hiatt, June Hemmons, The Principles of Knitting (Simon & Schuster, 1988)

Kooler, Donna, *Encyclopedia of Crochet* (Leisure Arts, 2002)

Righetti, Maggie, *Crocheting in Plain English* (St. Martin's Press, 1988)

Sims, Darla, *Crocheting for Fun & Profit* (Prima Publishing, 2000)

Thomas, Nancy J., Barnes & Nobles Basics: *Knitting and Crocheting,* (Barnes & Noble, 2004)

Tracy, Gloria and Susan Levin, *Crochet Your Way* (Taunton Press, 2000)

Turner, Pauline, *How to Crochet* (Collins & Brown, 2001)

Turner, Pauline. *Crocheted Lace* (Martingale & Company, 2003)

Measurements I Need to Know

(See pages 292–94 for advice on how to measure.)

Name

Bust/Chest

Center Back *(neck to cuff)*

Back Waist Length *(neck to waist)*

Cross Back *(shoulder to shoulder)*

Sleeve Length *(underarm to wrist)*

Head *(circumference)*

Name

Bust/Chest

Center Back *(neck to cuff)*

Back Waist Length *(neck to waist)*

Cross Back *(shoulder to shoulder)*

Sleeve Length *(underarm to wrist)*

Head *(circumference)*

Name

Bust/Chest

Center Back *(neck to cuff)*

Back Waist Length *(neck to waist)*

Cross Back *(shoulder to shoulder)*

Sleeve Length *(underarm to wrist)*

Head *(circumference)*

Name

Bust/Chest

Center Back *(neck to cuff)*

Back Waist Length *(neck to waist)*

Cross Back *(shoulder to shoulder)*

Sleeve Length *(underarm to wrist)*

Head *(circumference)*

Name

Bust/Chest

Center Back *(neck to cuff)*

Back Waist Length *(neck to waist)*

Cross Back *(shoulder to shoulder)*

Sleeve Length *(underarm to wrist)*

Head *(circumference)*

Name

Bust/Chest

Center Back *(neck to cuff)*

Back Waist Length *(neck to waist)*

Cross Back *(shoulder to shoulder)*

Sleeve Length *(underarm to wrist)*

Head *(circumference)*

Hook Inventory

METRIC	US	
.60 mm	14 steel	☐
.75	14 steel	☐
.85	13 steel	☐
1.00	12 steel	☐
1.1	11 steel	☐
1.25		☐
1.3	10 steel	☐
1.4	9 steel	☐
1.5	8 steel	☐
1.65	7 steel	☐
1.75, 1.8	6 steel	☐
1.9	5 steel	☐
2.0	4 steel	☐
2.1	3 steel	☐
2.25	2 steel, B/1	☐
2.5, 2.75	C/2	☐
3.0, 3.25	D/3	☐
3.5	E/4	☐
3.75, 4.0	F/5	☐
4.0, 4.25	G/6	☐
4.5	7	☐
5	H/8	☐
5.5	I/9	☐
6.0	J/10	☐
6.5, 7.0	K/10.5	☐
8	L/11	☐
9	M, N /13	☐
10	N, P /15	☐
15	P, Q	☐
16	Q	☐
19	S	☐

Index

Page numbers in *italics* indicate illustrations. Page numbers in **bold** indicate tables.

Z